MERRILL'S MARAUDERS

February – May 1944

MILITARY INSTRVCTION

CENTER OF MILITARY HISTORY

UNITED STATES ARMY

WASHINGTON, D.C. 1990

First printed by the Historical Division, War Department,
for the American Forces in Action series, 1945

CMH Pub 100–4

For sale by the Superintendent of Documents, U.S. Government Printing Office
Washington, D.C. 20402

Foreword to CMH Edition

Merrill's Marauders (February–May 1944) is one of a series of fourteen studies of World War II operations originally published by the War Department's Historical Division and now returned to print as part of the Army's commemoration of the fiftieth anniversary of that momentous clash of arms. These volumes, prepared by professional historians shortly after the events described, provide a concise summary of some of the major campaigns and battles fought by American soldiers. The skillful combination of combat interviews with primary sources, many of which are now lost, gives these unassuming narratives a special importance to military historians. The careful analysis of key operations provides numerous lessons for today's military students.

I am pleased that this entire group of studies will once again be available. I urge all military students and teachers to use them to enhance our collective awareness of the skill, leadership, daring, and professionalism exhibited by our military forebears.

Washington, D.C.
15 September 1989

HAROLD W. NELSON
Colonel, FA
Chief of Military History

Foreword

In the thick of battle, the soldier is busy doing his job. He has the knowledge and confidence that his job is part of a unified plan to defeat the enemy, but he does not have time to survey a campaign from a fox hole. If he should be wounded and removed behind the lines, he may have even less opportunity to learn what place he and his unit had in the larger fight.

AMERICAN FORCES IN ACTION is a series prepared by the War Department especially for the information of wounded men. It will show these soldiers, who have served their country so well, the part they and their comrades played in achievements which do honor to the record of the United States Army.

G. C. MARSHALL
Chief of Staff

WAR DEPARTMENT

Military Intelligence Division

Washington 25, D. C.

4 June 1945

Merrill's Marauders is an account of the operations of the 5307th Composite Unit (Provisional) in north Burma from February to May, 1944. The Marauders' effort was part of a coordinated offensive, the Allied reconquest of north Burma. Details of the offensive are summarized briefly to set the operations of the 5307th within the larger framework. On 10 August 1944 the 5307th was reorganized as the 475th Infantry Regiment.

The combat narrative is based mainly on interviews conducted by the historian of the 5307th after the operation and on information furnished the Historical Branch, G–2, War Department, by the Commanding General and several members of the unit. Few records were available because the Marauders restricted their files in order to maintain mobility while they were operating behind the Japanese lines. During the second mission a Japanese artillery shell scored a direct hit on the mule carrying the limited quantity of records and maps kept by the unit headquarters. During the third mission the heavy rains made preservation of papers impossible for more than a day or two. The unit's intelligence officer was killed at Myitkyina, and his records were washed away before they could be located.

This study is the fifth of a series called "American Forces in Action," designed exclusively for military personnel. No part of the narrative may be republished without the consent of the A.C. of S., G–2, War Department, Washington 25, D. C.

The manuscript was submitted by the Historical Section of the India-Burma Theater. One photograph is by Acme Newspictures, Inc. (page 25); three are by Capt. Logan E. Weston (pages 35, 63, 85); two aerials are by the U. S. Army Air Forces (pages 38; 104); all others are by the U. S. Army Signal Corps. Readers are urged to send directly to the Historical Branch, G–2, War Department, Washington 25, D. C., comments, criticisms, and additional information which may be of value in the preparation of a complete and definitive history of the operations of the 5307th Composite Unit (Provisional).

Contents

Illustrations

Maps

Sketches

MAP NO. 1

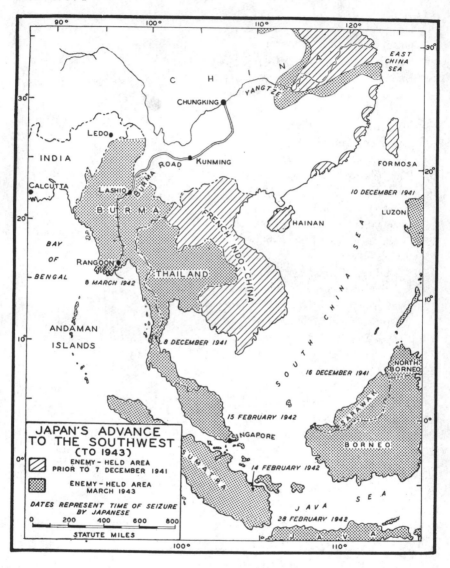

JAPAN'S ADVANCE
TO THE SOUTHWEST
(TO 1943)

ENEMY-HELD AREA
PRIOR TO 7 DECEMBER 1941

ENEMY-HELD AREA
MARCH 1943

DATES REPRESENT TIME OF SEIZURE
BY JAPANESE

0   200   400   600   800

STATUTE MILES

Introduction

THE 5307th COMPOSITE UNIT (Provisional) of the Army of the United States was organized and trained for long-range penetration behind enemy lines in Japanese-held Burma. Commanded by Brig. Gen. (now Maj. Gen.) Frank D. Merrill, its 2,997 officers and men became popularly known as "Merrill's Marauders." From February to May, 1944 the operations of the Marauders were closely coordinated with those of the Chinese 22d and 38th Divisions in a drive to recover northern Burma and clear the way for the construction of the Ledo Road, which was to link the Indian railhead at Ledo with the old Burma Road to China. The Marauders were foot soldiers who marched and fought through jungles and over mountains from the Hukawng Valley in northwestern Burma to Myitkyina on the Irrawaddy River. In 5 major and 30 minor engagements they met and defeated the veteran soldiers of the Japanese 18th Division. Operating in the rear of the main forces of the Japanese, they prepared the way for the southward advance of the Chinese by disorganizing supply lines and communications. The climax of the Marauders' operations was the capture of the Myitkyina airfield, the only all-weather strip in northern Burma. This was the final victory of the 5307th Composite Unit, which was disbanded in August, 1944.

The War in Burma, January, 1942 — March, 1943

Burma had been conquered by the Japanese 2 years before the Marauders' operations (Map No. 1, opposite). During the 6 months

BRIG. GEN. FRANK D. MERRILL
Commanding General, 5307th Composite Unit (Provisional)

2

between December, 1941 and May, 1942 the enemy had overrun the Philippines, much of Oceania, all of the Netherlands East Indies, all of the Malay Peninsula, and almost all of Burma. In the Pacific Ocean his advance threatened communications between the United States and Australasia. On the Asiatic mainland his occupation of Burma menaced India, provided a bulwark against counterattack from the west, cut the last land route for supply of China, and added Burma's raw materials to the resources of an empire already rich.

For the conquest of Burma the Japanese had concentrated two divisions in southern Thailand (Map No. 2, page 4). In mid-January, 1942 they struck toward Moulmein, which fell on the 30th. British, Indian, and Burmese forces, aided by the Royal Air Force and the American Volunteer Group, resisted the Salween and Sittang river crossings but were overwhelmed by enemy superiority in numbers, equipment, and planes. Rangoon, the capital and principal port, was taken on 8 March. The Japanese then turned north in two columns. One division pushed up the Sittang where Chinese forces under Maj. Gen. (now General) Joseph W. Stilwell were coming in to defend the Burma Road.[1] The other Japanese division pursued the Indian and Burmese forces up the Irrawaddy Valley. On 1 and 2 April, the enemy took Toungoo on the Sittang and Prome on the Irrawaddy. From Yenangyaung, north of Prome, a column pushed westward and on 4 May took the port of Akyab on the Bay of Bengal. The conquest of southern Burma was complete.

A third enemy column of two divisions, which had landed at Rangoon on 12 April 1942, was now attacking on the east from the Shan States into the upper Salween Valley and driving rapidly northward to take Lashio, junction of the rail and highway sections of the Burma Road. Mandalay, completely outflanked, was evacuated by its Chinese defenders and occupied by the Japanese on 1 May. From Lashio the Japanese pushed up the Salween Valley well into the Chinese province of Yunnan. In north central Burma they sent a small patrol northward along the Irrawaddy almost to Fort Hertz, and to the west they took Kalewa on the Chindwin. The main rem-

---

[1] The "Burma Road" extends from Rangoon to Chungking, approximately 1,445 miles. It is actually made up of a railroad from Rangoon to Lashio, a new motor road from Lashio to Kunming, and an old highway from Kunming to Chungking. The new section, constructed in 2 years from 1937–39, was the first link between Burma and China for heavy traffic. Before the Japanese conquest of Burma, the road carried vital supplies to the Chinese armies fighting the Japanese. Great Britain, acceding to a request from Japan, closed the route from July to October, 1940 but reopened it when Japan joined the Rome-Berlin axis.

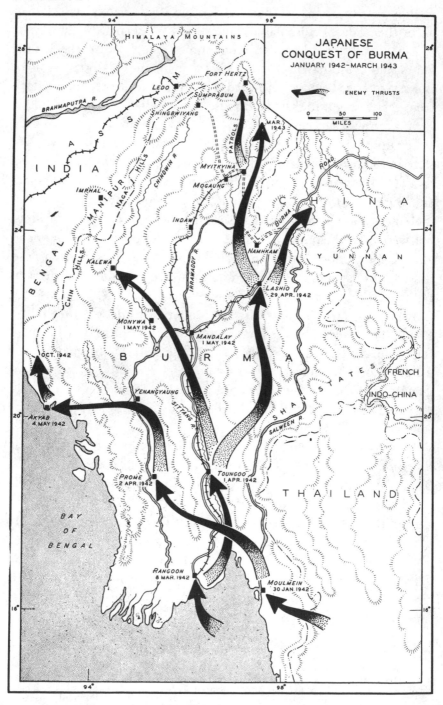

JAPANESE
CONQUEST OF BURMA
JANUARY 1942-MARCH 1943

ENEMY THRUSTS

0   50   100
MILES

4

nants of General Stilwell's forces retired from north Burma to India by way of Shingbwiyang, while British, Burmese, and Indian survivors withdrew up the valley of the Chindwin and across the Chin Hills. The Allied withdrawal was made on foot, for no motor road or railway connected India with Burma.

When the monsoon rains came in June the Japanese held all of Burma except for fringes of mountain, jungle, and swamp on the north and west. General Stilwell grimly summarized the campaign: "I claim we got a hell-of-a-beating. We got run out of Burma, and it is as humiliating as hell. I think we ought to find out what caused it, go back, and retake it." But this counteroffensive could not start at once, and the Japanese were able to make further advances in the next fighting season.

At the end of October they pushed northwestward along the coast from Akyab toward Bengal. Approximately a month later British forces counterattacked strongly along this same coast, but their gains could not be held, and the Japanese force reached the frontier of Bengal. In February of the next year the enemy began to drive northward from Myitkyina. He had covered some 75 air miles by early March and was closing in on Sumprabum, threatening to occupy the whole of northern Burma and to destroy the British-led Kachin and Gurkha levies which had hitherto dominated the area. The Allies were in no position to stop this advance. Their regular forces had retired from the area to India in May and were separated from the Japanese by densely forested mountain ranges and malarial valleys.

The enemy was apparently secure in Southeast Asia. The question of the moment was whether his advance would halt at the Burma border or would continue into India.

From Defense to Offense

The strategic situation in Burma began to change in the spring of 1943 when the Allies assumed the offensive with an experimental operation behind the enemy lines (Map No. 3, page 6). This operation, foreshadowing the part the Marauders were to take in the larger offensive of 1944, was an expedition commanded by Maj. Gen. (then Brigadier) Orde C. Wingate, who led long-range-penetration units of the 77 Indian Infantry Brigade across the natural barrier between India and Burma into Japanese-held territory.

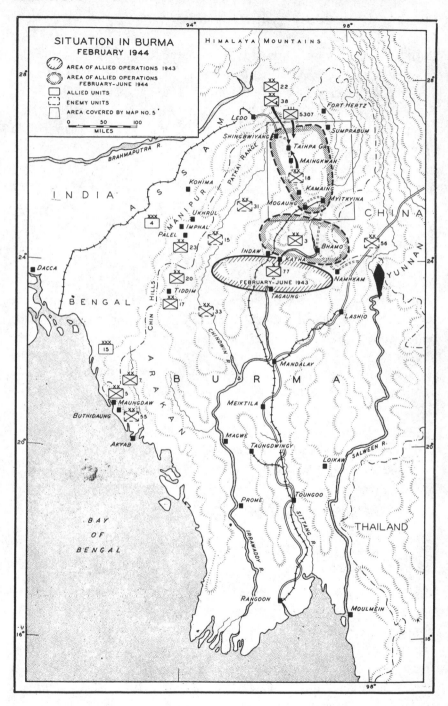

SITUATION IN BURMA
FEBRUARY 1944

AREA OF ALLIED OPERATIONS 1943
AREA OF ALLIED OPERATIONS
FEBRUARY–JUNE 1944
ALLIED UNITS
ENEMY UNITS
AREA COVERED BY MAP NO. 5

0   50   100
MILES

Wingate's forces consisted of eight jungle columns totaling 3,200 men, assembled from British, Indian, Burmese, and Gurkha troops. Directed by radio and supplied by air drops, in a period of 4 months (February to June, 1943) his columns covered a distance of 1,000 miles. In the area of northern Burma, from the Chindwin River eastward to China, they gathered topographical and other intelligence, harassed and confused the Japanese forces, and cut enemy lines of communication. The columns put the Mandalay-Myitkyina railway out of action for 4 weeks and engrossed the efforts of six to eight enemy battalions. When ordered to return, the columns dispersed in small groups, each of which successfully fought its own way out of Burma.

After this first penetration the seasonal rains again restricted ground activity. However, Allied bombers of the Tenth Air Force continued their attacks on Japanese supply lines in both Burma and Thailand with steadily increasing strength. Maj. Gen. George E. Stratemeyer's force had established definite superiority over Burma by November, 1943, the beginning of the dry season during which a ground offensive was possible.

At this time many indications pointed to a resumption of the Japanese offensive against India. Since the fall of 1942 the enemy had brought two more divisions into the area, making a total of five distributed along the India border. The one division (55th) on the front beyond Akyab was extremely aggressive. In the Chin Hills three others (the 15th, 31st, and 33d) were organizing for a strong offensive into Manipur Province. The 18th Division, in northern Burma, was ready to oppose any advance from Assam.

The Allies, too, were preparing for major offensive operations from both India and China. Admiral Lord Louis Mountbatten,[2] commander in Southeast Asia, was assembling troops and supplies in Bengal and Manipur. Generalissimo Chiang Kai-shek was strengthening his forces along the Salween River in Yunnan. The first Allied blow was to come from the north, led by General Stilwell, Deputy Commander in the Southeast Asia Command and Chief of Staff for Allied operations in the Chinese theater. Operating from bases in the upper Brahmaputra Valley, General Stilwell had mounted an offensive to carry over the Patkai Range, conquer northern Burma,

[2] Admiral Mountbatten was appointed Supreme Allied Commander, Southeast Asia Command, at the Quebec Conference of August, 1943.

7

and open a new land route to China. American-trained Chinese divisions constituted his main striking force. In immediate support of his advance, long-range-penetration operations were to be carried out by combat teams of the 5307th Composite Unit (Provisional) under General Merrill.

By February, when the 5307th arrived in the area of operations, General Stilwell's offensive had made good progress. The Chinese 22d and 38th Divisions had crossed the Patkai barrier and were engaging the Japanese forces in the flood plains of the Hukawng Valley. Covered by this advance, United States engineers had pushed a road over the Patkais to Shingbwiyang, 100 miles from the starting base at Ledo. However, the main enemy resistance and strongest prepared positions were still to be met.

Secondary Allied operations had been planned to support the main drive into north Burma. General Wingate's jungle columns of the 3 Indian Division were ready to thrust into central Burma, with the aim of cutting enemy communications far south of General Stilwell's objectives. On the Irrawaddy headwaters in northeast Burma the Allies had a base at Fort Hertz, in wild country which the Japanese had never been able to conquer. Here, Gurkha and Kachin levies from the native tribes were harassing Japanese outposts in the Sumprabum-Myitkyina corridor.

Origin and Training of the American Force

The 5307th Composite Unit (Provisional) was organized to participate in the Burma operations as the result of a decision made at the Quebec Conference in August, 1943. Five months later, on 1 February 1944, the three battalions comprising the provisional unit had been transported to India, organized, trained, and equipped for employment. They were the only American ground combat troops designated at this time for the China-Burma-India Theater.

On 1 September 1943, when the size of the battalions had been fixed at 1,000, the War Department began recruiting personnel from jungle-trained and jungle-tested troops, primarily infantrymen. General George C. Marshall requested 300 volunteers "of a high state of physical ruggedness and stamina" from the Southwest Pacific, 700 from the South Pacific, and 1,000 each from the Caribbean Defense Command and the Army Ground Forces in the United States.

COL. CHARLES N. HUNTER
Second in Command
5307th Composite Unit (Provisional)

DEOGARH TRAINING CAMP, *set up late in November, 1943, was occupied by the Marauders for more than two months.*

In answer to General Marshall's request the South and Southwest Pacific commands selected 950 men from veterans of Guadalcanal, New Guinea, and other operations in those theaters. The Caribbean Defense Command secured 950 more troops who had served on Trinidad and Puerto Rico, and a similar number came from highly trained units within the United States. The Caribbean volunteers flew to Miami, crossed the continent by rail, and assembled in San Francisco with the volunteers from the States. These men formed two battalions; the third from the South and Southwest Pacific areas was to join the force on the way to Bombay.

Col. Charles N. Hunter, the senior officer among the volunteers, was appointed commander of the battalions. He was ordered to prepare the men while en route for the performance of their mission, to keep General Stilwell informed of the progress of the movement, and to report to the General upon arrival in the theater.

On 21 September, the two battalions sailed from San Francisco on the *Lurline*. As much of their equipment as could be loaded aboard went with them; the remainder was sent to San Diego, and from there it was to be forwarded in one shipment to Bombay.[3] The *Lurline* proceeded to Noumea, New Caledonia, where 650 officers and men from the South Pacific Theater came aboard. The contingent from the Southwest Pacific joined the ship at Brisbane, Australia. After a brief stop at Perth, the *Lurline* steamed across the Indian Ocean and up the Arabian Sea to Bombay, where the three battalions disembarked by 31 October.

Organizing and training of the 5307th began immediately. Col. (now Brig. Gen.) Francis G. Brink, selected because he had trained Chinese troops in India, instructed the unit in long-range-penetration tactics. After meeting the *Lurline* at Bombay, he accompanied the troops to a British camp at Deolali and 3 weeks later moved with them to Deogarh, close to an area suitable for jungle training.

From the end of November, 1943 to the end of January, 1944 the 5307th remained at Deogarh and trained intensively. On the advice of General Wingate, who supervised the over-all preparation of the unit, each battalion was formed into two jungle columns, called "combat teams" by the Americans. These were not combat teams in the accepted American sense, for their organization represented only a division of each battalion into two smaller units, without any addition of elements not organic to the battalion. The division was made in such a manner that each "combat team" had its share of the heavy weapons and other organic battalion elements and thus was able to operate as a self-contained unit (Chart, page 14).

Lt. Col. William L. Osborne was assigned command of the 1st Battalion, and its two combat teams, Red and White, were placed under Maj. Edward M. Ghiz and Maj. Caifson Johnson, respectively (Chart, page 12). Lt. Col. George A. McGee, Jr., became commanding officer of the 2d Battalion, which was composed of Blue Combat Team under Maj. Richard W. Healy and Green Combat Team under Capt. Thomas E. Bogardus. The 3d Battalion was placed under command of Lt. Col. Charles E. Beach and comprised Orange Combat Team under Maj. Lawrence L. Lew and Khaki Combat Team under Maj. Edwin J. Briggs.

---

[3] Almost all equipment had arrived before the troops started up the Ledo Road. Among the essential pieces lacking were Browning automatic rifle clips, which were supplied to the unit from theater stock.

ORGANIZATION OF THE 5307TH COMPOSITE UNIT (PROVISIONAL)

TO 27 APRIL 1944

COMMAND POST GROUP
Executive Officer
Maj. Louis J. Williams

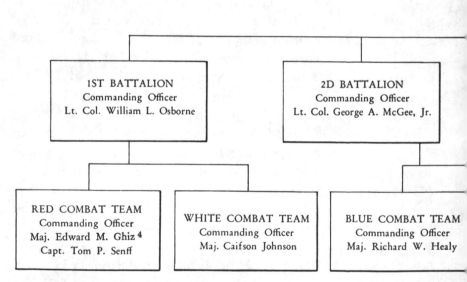

1ST BATTALION
Commanding Officer
Lt. Col. William L. Osborne

2D BATTALION
Commanding Officer
Lt. Col. George A. McGee, Jr.

RED COMBAT TEAM
Commanding Officer
Maj. Edward M. Ghiz [4]
Capt. Tom P. Senff

WHITE COMBAT TEAM
Commanding Officer
Maj. Caifson Johnson

BLUE COMBAT TEAM
Commanding Officer
Maj. Richard W. Healy

[4] Commanding Officer to 6 April 1944.

[5] Commanding Officer to 4 April 1944.

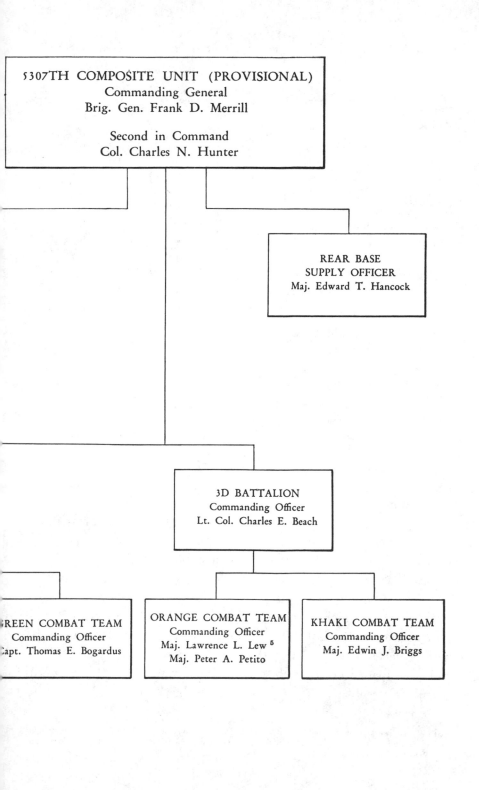

5307TH COMPOSITE UNIT (PROVISIONAL)
Commanding General
Brig. Gen. Frank D. Merrill

Second in Command
Col. Charles N. Hunter

REAR BASE
SUPPLY OFFICER
Maj. Edward T. Hancock

3D BATTALION
Commanding Officer
Lt. Col. Charles E. Beach

GREEN COMBAT TEAM
Commanding Officer
Capt. Thomas E. Bogardus

ORANGE COMBAT TEAM
Commanding Officer
Maj. Lawrence L. Lew [5]
Maj. Peter A. Petito

KHAKI COMBAT TEAM
Commanding Officer
Maj. Edwin J. Briggs

ORGANIZATION OF BATTALIONS
(This Table of Organization does not include supply base detachment at Dinjan.)

	Battalion Headquarters	Combat teams No. 1	Combat teams No. 2	Total
Officers	3	16	16	35
Enlisted men	13	456	459	928
Aggregate	16	472	475	963
Animals (horses and mules) ..	3	68	68	139
Carbines	6	86	89	181
Machine guns, Heavy		3	4	7
Machine guns, Light		2	4	6
Machine guns, Sub	2	52	48	102
Mortars, 60-mm		4	6	10
Mortars, 81-mm		4	3	7
Pistols		2	2	4
Rifles, Browning Automatic....		27	27	54
Rifles, M–1	8	306	310	624
Rockets		3	3	6

General Composition of each Combat Team:[6]

 Headquarters Platoon
 Intelligence and Reconnaissance Platoon
 Pioneer and Demolition Platoon
 Medical Detachment
 Heavy Weapons Platoon (3 heavy machine guns, 4 81-mm mortars)
 1½ Rifle Companies
 ½ Company Headquarters

Colonel Brink, assisted by Lt. Col. Daniel E. Still, delegated supervision of training to the battalion commanders, who were encouraged to add their own ideas to the program. For slightly more than 2 months they prepared the men for the problems of operating in dense tropical jungles defended by a stubborn and skillful enemy.

Individual training emphasized marksmanship, scouting and patrolling, map reading, and jungle navigation. A normal amount of calisthenics was included in the daily routine, and the length and pace of marches were increased in order to make the men physically hard. Classes always marched to and from ranges and training areas, no matter how far they were from camp. Packs were worn whenever possible.

---

[6] Each battalion commander arranged a division of his organization into combat teams, so that only a general table of composite parts can be given here. For instance, the 1st Battalion was so divided that one combat team had a rifle company and rifle company headquarters and the other combat team had two rifle companies.

Platoon tactics were stressed in every training operation. Company, combat team, battalion, and unit exercises were also held, but time was short and attention had to be directed mostly toward moulding squads and platoons into highly efficient and well-coordinated teams. Each small unit was familiarized as much as possible with the normal combat activities of other types of units. Rifle platoon leaders and noncommissioned officers were instructed in directing mortar fire, and all men were taught the rudiments of voice radio procedure.

In general, the heavy weapons, intelligence and reconnaissance, pioneer and demolition, and communications personnel were already

TEN MILES A DAY *was the average rate of movement over the Ledo Road for the Marauder column.*

well trained in their special functions. Taking part in all training of their combat teams, they became physically hardened to the same extent as the rest of the men. Rear echelon personnel, including parachute packers, riggers, and kick-out crews, were trained separately by the unit S–4.

Ten days spent on maneuvers with General Wingate's troops brought to light minor deficiencies. There was a shortage of pack animals, and the changes which had been made in organization and equipment required final adjustments.

After the commanders within the unit had been assigned, General Merrill was placed in charge of the entire force. He appointed Maj. Louis J. Williams as his executive officer, in charge of the Command Post group.

On 8 January 1944, the completely organized and trained unit was assigned to General Stilwell's field command in northern Burma.[7] He expected to use it in conjunction with the Chinese forces which were beginning their drive against the Japanese 18th Division. In accordance with General Stilwell's concept of the use of long-range-penetration units, the 5307th was to be sent on bold missions against assigned objectives behind the enemy lines in order to facilitate the seizure of key points by the main Chinese forces.

General Stilwell's immediate orders to the 5307th were to close in on Ledo by 7 February and from there to march over the trail as far as Ningbyen. The unit started at once from the training area in order to arrive on schedule. The 1,000-mile trip by train and boat to Ledo consumed a month; the last 100 miles on foot took 10 days. On 19 February the 1st Battalion, head of the column, arrived at Ningbyen. It was followed 2 days later by the 3d Battalion, tail of the column. The men had been thoroughly tested by the 10-day march and were ready for their first assignment.

Area of Operations

Plans for the Ledo Road [8] are the key to an understanding of the 1944 campaign in northern Burma (Map No. 4, page 17). Reopening land communications with China had become a main aim of Allied

---

[7] The 31st and 33d Quartermaster Pack Troops, a detachment of the 835th Signal Service Battalion, and a platoon of the 502d Military Police Battalion were added to the unit early in January.

[8] On 28 January 1945 Generalissimo Chiang Kai-shek, announcing the completion of the Ledo-Burma Road, renamed the 1,044-mile route to China the "Stilwell Road" in honor of General Stilwell. The first Allied convoy was on its way from Ledo to Kumming.

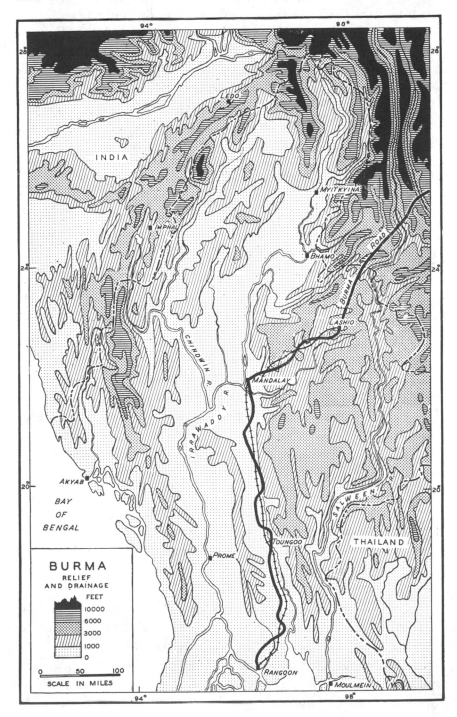

BURMA
RELIEF
AND DRAINAGE
FEET
10000
6000
3000
1000
0

0   50   100
SCALE IN MILES

strategy, but only the total reconquest of Burma would give the Allies control of the old route from Rangoon. The Ledo Road constituted a daring effort to drive a new route from northeast India across north Burma, tapping the Burma Road at the frontier of China. The base of departure, at Ledo in the Brahmaputra Valley, had rail and water connections with Bengal. Nearly 300 air miles separated Ledo from the projected point of link-up with the Burma Road near Bhamo.

The plans for the Ledo Road included the laying of pipe lines, designed to relieve the road and air traffic of carrying fuel from Assam to China. Once the construction of the road was settled, it was decided that two 4-inch lines from Tinsukia, 30 air miles northwest of Ledo, would follow the road. They were to be fed by gasoline pumped from Calcutta to a station near their starting point.

Military conquest of north Burma was a prerequisite for operations of the engineers, and for either infantry or engineers, the area presented major difficulties in terrain and climate. Abutting to the north on the impassable ranges of the Himalayas, where peaks rise to 20,000 feet, north Burma is separated both from India and China by massive frontier mountains. On the India side, a continuous range runs southwest from the Himalayas along the Assam border in parallel ridges reaching heights of 10,000 feet; in the Patkai portion of this range, southeast of Ledo, the Pangsau Pass at about 4,300 feet leads into Burma, making a gateway for the projected road. On the east, the Himalayas curve south along the China frontier to the region of Bhamo. Boxed in on three sides by these main barriers, north Burma is essentially a rugged hill country divided into two compartments by the north-south Kumon Range, with elevations over 10,000 feet. To the east of the Kumons, the Irrawaddy pushes a narrow valley north from Myitkyina into the Himalayas; Sumprabum was the main enemy outpost in this valley. In the other compartment, the headwaters of the Chindwin River have carved out fairly extensive lowlands in the hill country; one of these plains, the Hukawng Valley, lies near the Pangsau Pass over the Patkai Range. Reference to the physiographic map (Map No. 5, page 19) will show the geographic features that governed both the plans for the Ledo Road and the plans for the military operations that would clear the way for this new route to China. Once over the Patkai Range, the essential problem was to get from the Hukawng lowlands over into the upper Irrawaddy

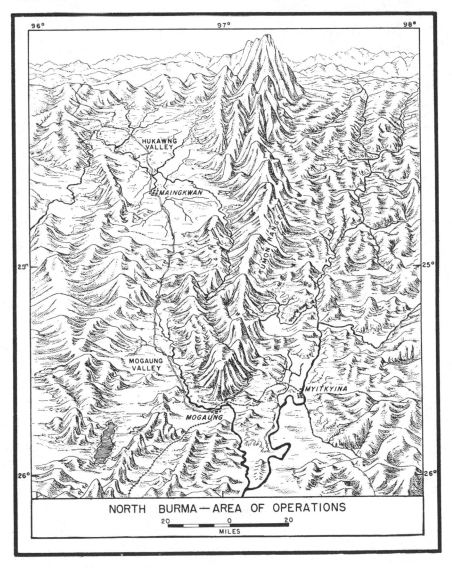

96° 97° 98°

HUKAWNG
VALLEY

SHMAINGKWAN

KUMON RANGE

25° 25°

MOGAUNG
VALLEY

MYITKYINA

MOGAUNG

26° 26°

NORTH BURMA—AREA OF OPERATIONS

20 0 20
MILES

plains near Myitkyina. The best route was by a natural corridor, the narrow Mogaung Valley. This skirted the southwest side of the Kumon Mountains, then passed between them and the lower hills to the southwest to reach a tributary of the Irrawaddy River.

It was in this area of about 5,000 square miles, roughly the size of Connecticut, that the Marauders were to operate. When the three battalions of the 5307th arrived at Ningbyen, they had marched through a typical portion of north Burma and had experienced the regional conditions under which they were to fight. They had struggled over the ridges of the Patkai Range, where, even in the relatively low country of the pass, they doubted whether "those goddam hills would ever level out." They had been impressed by the tropical rain forests characteristic of western mountain slopes in Burma, where trees 20 feet in diameter at the base rose straight and clean of branches to a dense roof of foliage at 80 or 100 feet. Brush was scant in the gloom of these forests, but the footing was poor in a mould of rotting vegetation 3 to 4 feet deep. In the Hukawng lowlands, the Marauders entered the typical jungle country of north Burma, and veterans of Guadalcanal soon learned that this jungle outmatched that of the Solomon Islands for difficulty. Trees were smaller and more scattered than in the mountains, permitting a rank growth of underbrush, often briary and tangled with vines. Patches of bamboo were sometimes so dense that to chop a trail involved cutting away the lower part of the growth to make a tunnel under the matted plant tops. Growth in the occasional clearings might consist of kunai ("elephant") grass, 4 to 6 feet high and sharp-edged. Everywhere in this country, whether on hills or in the river flood plains, men found that their clothes were damp all the time, even in the driest period of the year, and that their weapons rusted if not disassembled and oiled daily.

In a country of many large and small streams, heavy jungle, and rough hills, the problems of movement and transportation were made even more difficult by the absence of roads. North Burma is an undeveloped frontier country, and native footpaths and cart tracks provided the only means of communication in most of the area. The one road suitable for motor traffic, and then only in the dry months, ran north from Kamaing via the Mogaung corridor and into the Hukawng plain. The nearest railhead was at Myitkyina, reached by a single-track line connecting with central and southern Burma.

Burma has a tropical monsoon climate with clearly marked wet and dry seasons. From June to the end of September the moisture-laden southwest monsoon brings extremely heavy rains to the western and southern flanks of the highlands; annual precipitation on the westernmost hills varies from 150 to 250 inches. In northern Burma, slopes which face the monsoon also receive abundant rain, ranging

AT THE HALFWAY MARK ON THE LEDO ROAD, *the men of the 5307th wind downhill through the Patkai Range.*

between 75 and 100 inches. In the months from January to April, many of the innumerable small streams dry up, and only the large rivers present difficulties for crossing. During the wet period, lowlands such as the Hukawng Valley and even the Mogaung corridor are flooded to the point where movement is greatly restricted; the Ledo Road was to provide the first all-weather route that northern Burma had seen. Temperatures are high throughout the year at lower altitudes but from October to February are not excessive, ranging from 60° to 90° in the lowlands, and during these months the weather is clear and pleasant. Though the dry season does not end until June, the weather becomes increasingly hot and humid from March until the monsoon rains finally break.

The heavily forested hills and valleys of north Burma are thinly populated by pagan Kachins, who have lived in almost complete independence of the government in Rangoon. In 1931 Myitkyina, the largest town, had only 7,328 people in comparison with Mandalay's 134,950 and Rangoon's 398,967. Localities named on maps in territory where the Marauders operated might turn out to be less than hamlets; Lagang Ga has fewer than five houses, and Inkangahtawng, only a jungle clearing, has not a single basha (hut). The settlements usually consist of from 12 to 100 or more huts, built of timber uprights and bamboo. To protect the inhabitants against wild animals the villages are often surrounded by bamboo and wooden stockades. Many of the primitive tribesmen living in this area first came into contact with people of the outside world when their country became a battle-ground for Allied and Japanese armies.

The vegetation in north Burma is limited almost entirely to large trees and dense underbrush. Wild nuts, fruit, or edible growths, usually found in quantities in jungle areas, are rare in the Hukawng and Mogaung valleys. In small clearings around the villages only enough rice is raised to provide food for the local inhabitants. Cultivated areas increase as southern Burma is approached, where the densely populated valleys and coastal plains show an intricate pattern of paddies producing the great staple crop of the country.

The Kachins are active as traders and mine the amber and jade found in the Hukawng Valley and around Myitkyina. They practice nature worship, in contrast to the Buddhism of the more civilized Burmans who occupy the lowlands to the south. When organized by Americans and British, the Kachins proved very helpful as guides and auxiliary troops in the campaign against the Japanese.

In the hot and humid climate of Burma, disease was a greater peril to our men than the enemy. Almost everywhere malaria and dysentery were endemic. Many of the volunteers from the Pacific theaters had malaria before they reached India, and very few men were uninfected by the end of the campaign. Immunization treatments were not effective against a variety of typhus fever, communicated by mites. The Marauders' long and exhausting marches in rain and tropical heat, their inadequate nourishment, and their inability to take even the simplest precautions against infection resulted in a high percentage of casualties from disease.

The mountains, forests, and rivers of north Burma often seemed imposing and sometimes beautiful to our men. But hard experience proved that the land was no tropical paradise. It literally swarmed with enemies. Diseases and hardships of war in the jungle combined to sap the strength of the Marauders until they reached Myitkyina too exhausted to continue as a fighting force.

Supply

Normal methods of supply were impractical for a highly mobile force operating behind the enemy's forward defensive positions. Any attempts to maintain regular land supply lines, even if adequate roads had been available, would have greatly reduced tactical mobility and would have made secrecy impossible, contradicting the express purposes of the operation. Air dropping of food and munitions, though still in an experimental stage of development, had been satisfactory for General Wingate's expedition of 1943 and was adopted for the long-range-penetration missions of the Marauders.

The experience of General Wingate's expedition had disclosed both the possibilities of air supply and the major difficulties to be overcome. Adequate air and radio equipment, as well as competent air liaison and communications personnel, were absolute essentials. If air supply was to be a success it had to be planned with the utmost care and foresight. Adequate quantities of supplies had to be available at a base for shipment on a moment's notice. Means must be provided for accurate and quick radio communication between the units in the field and the supply base, since exact information regarding requirements, dropping area, and time of drop was necessary. Correct and careful packaging and loading of the supplies, whether to be dropped with or without parachutes, were required if safe delivery was to be assured. The actual dropping called for skilled pilots and crews who could approximate low-level bombing accuracy over the small jungle fields. Cargo planes had to be of types suitable for the kind of work anticipated, and fighter protection was necessary because interference by enemy planes was to be expected. Success would depend on attainment of the closest cooperation between air and ground forces. Air force and supply personnel had to realize that the outcome of the whole enterprise was completely dependent on teamwork of the highest order. The needs of the ground troops for food and ammunition could not wait on good flying conditions.

SUPPLY DROPS *were received at about thirty areas during the operation. Here a C-47 releases its parachutes over a jungle clearing, marked with panels.*

Bamboo warehouses at Dinjan, 32 miles west of Ledo, were made available to Maj. Edward T. Hancock, supply officer for the 5307th. Good air strips were nearby at Chabua, Tinsukia, and Sookerating. Arrangements were made for coded communication by SCR 284 from General Merrill's headquarters to Dinjan through Combat Headquarters at Ledo. Eventually the base at Dinjan monitored all messages from General Merrill to Headquarters, thus eliminating the loss of time involved in relaying requisitions. Standard units of each category of supplies, based on estimated requirements for 1 day, were packaged ready for delivery. Requisitions were submitted on a basis covering daily needs or were readily adapted to this basis.

At the beginning of the Marauders' operation the 2d Troop Carrier Squadron and later the 1st Troop Carrier Squadron carried the supplies from the Dinjan base to forward drop areas. They dropped by parachute engineering equipment, ammunition, medical supplies, and food from an altitude of about 200 feet; clothing and grain were dropped without parachute from 150 feet. They flew in all kinds of weather. During March alone, in 17 missions averaging 6 to 7 planes, they ferried into the combat area 376 tons of supplies.

The squadrons using C–47's had only one complaint about their transports. Because the planes lacked a drop port in the floor, the supplies, "kicked" out of the side door, sometimes struck the left horizontal stabilizer if the pilot could not maintain level flight. One plane was lost and two were damaged by parachutes catching on the stabilizer. Fighter protection was seldom requested for the drop planes, and only two were lost by enemy action during the campaign.

Where no open space or paddy field was available for the drop, it was necessary to prepare a field, but in the majority of cases the route of march and the supply requirements could be so coordinated that units were near some suitable flat, open area when drops were needed.

MARAUDERS CLEAR THE DROP FIELD. *One man packs clover-leaf ammunition containers, while other men carry the rest of the supplies from the field to a distribution point.*

This was an advantage, not only because it relieved the troops of the hard work of clearing ground, but because it enabled the pilots to use aerial photographs and maps to identify their destinations.

The packages, attached to A–4 and A–7 parachutes,[9] weighed between 115 and 125 pounds. Containers of this size were easily manhandled. As soon as they reached the ground, two of them were loaded on a mule and transported to a distributing point in a relatively secure area. There they were opened and the men filed by, each one picking up an individual package of rations or ammunition. Rations, wrapped in a burlap bag, contained food, salt tablets, cigarettes, and occasionally halazone tablets for purifying drinking water.

The rations delivered to the Marauders were 80 percent "K," 5 percent "C," 5 percent "10-in-1," and 10 percent "B." A variety in this diet was provided only once when the rear echelon prepared a mess of fried chicken and apple turnovers which was dropped to the 2d Battalion during its darkest days at Nhpum Ga.

When the situation permitted, the practice was to send back to the Dinjan base in the evening the radio request for supplies to be dropped the following afternoon. In emergency cases the service could be speeded up. Special material not available at the Dinjan base was sometimes procured, transported, and dropped 12 hours after the original request was made. The shortest time for a supply mission was recorded on 6 May when a C–47 reached the drop area, 128 miles from Dinjan, just 2 hours and 22 minutes after the message had been filed in the field.

Tabulations were prepared for determining readily the weight of each delivery so that the air liaison officer would know how many planes were needed at any time. A situation map, posted in Major Hancock's office, was kept up to date, and, in a number of instances, anticipatory planning was carried to such an extent that ammunition was actually loaded on trucks kept ready to dash for the airfield. At the destination, air-ground communication with the unit being supplied was used to achieve the greatest possible coordination of effort.

---

[9] The A–4 is a canvas container approximately 12″ x 24″ x 30″ inclosed in a reinforced webbing harness and lined with two corrugated pasteboard boxes. The parachute is attached to the webbing harness. This container is used primarily for dropping of medical supplies, signal equipment, and other similar semifragile cargo.

The A–7 consists of two 6-foot adjustable webbing straps sewn together at right angles to inclose boxes of supplies. The parachute is attached at the junction of the two straps. This container is used for dropping small-arms ammunition and other items of a durable nature.

Careful planning, supplemented by speedy adoption of lessons learned from experience, paid big dividends in terms of efficient operation of the air supply system. About 250 enlisted members of the 5307th, including packers, riggers, drivers, and food droppers, were responsible for the job; everyone realized the importance of his role and felt a personal obligation to get the supplies to his comrades in the field at the time and place and in the quantities required. Major Hancock, commander of the base detachment, was assisted by Capt. Willard C. Nelson who was executive officer, Lt. Robert O. Gardiner who supervised the packing of parachutes, and 1st Lt. Marlan E. Lowell who handled air liaison. These officers and their enlisted personnel never allowed any obstacle to interfere with the delivery of supplies. Their outstanding performance and that of pilots and air crews resulted in a smoothly functioning supply system. The high degree of mobility and secrecy which resulted from air supply was one of the chief reasons for the success of the Marauders.

L-4's EVACUATED WOUNDED FROM FORWARD STRIPS. *This liaison plane carries a casualty from Hsamshingyang to a rear field.*

AN AMBULANCE PLANE *transports wounded Chinese and American soldiers from a rear field to a hospital in the Ledo area.*

Evacuation of Casualties

The 71st Liaison Squadron, using L-4's and L-5's based at Ledo, evacuated the great majority of Marauder casualties from the combat zone after they had been treated by Medical corpsmen or surgical teams. The light liaison planes, landing on drop areas, rice paddies, or gravel bars along the rivers, flew the wounded, often within a period of a few hours after injury, to rear air strips or to collecting and clearing companies along the Ledo Road. From the air strips, ambulance planes (C-47's) transported the casualties to the 20th General Hospital, the 14th Evacuation Hospital, or the 111th Station Hospital in the Ledo area. After the capture of Myitkyina airfield both C-46's and C–47's, landing on the strip, were regularly assigned to evacuating Americans. Speed in carrying the wounded where they could receive hospital treatment saved the lives of many men who could not have withstood the journey overland through the jungle.

Communications

Before entering the area of operations, the 5307th arranged to carry long- and short-range radios providing constant communication with higher headquarters for orders, supply arrangements, and air cooperation, and within the unit itself for control of the columns. Since the battalions were to be always on the move and most of the time behind enemy lines, it was necessary to carry wherever they went even the heavier, more powerful radio sets. They left Ledo equipped with six radios (three long-range AN/PRC–1's and three SCR 284's) [10] mounted on mules. Each battalion had an AN/PRC–1, for communication to the base station at Dinjan and to the liaison station at General Stilwell's forward headquarters, and an SCR 284 (20-mile range), for signaling transport and fighter planes flying missions for the ground troops. During the latter part of the operation the unit used an SCR 177–S,[11] converted for mule pack, to contact rear and forward units and the temporary command base then located at Naubum. From Ledo to Myitkyina all headquarters within the battalions had SCR 300's (Walkie-Talkie).[12] Since this voice instrument proved most reliable for distances up to 3 and sometimes 10 miles in level country, the headquarters used it for quick column contact, supplementing their runners. Except on long marches, the men packed these 32-pound sets on their backs to relay information about enemy movements and to direct mortar and artillery fire.

The communications men found the long-range radios more difficult to transport and operate satisfactorily. These powerful sets required from one to three mules for carriage; their range was limited by the dense jungle growth and the uneven terrain, and they func-

---

[10] The AN/PRC–1 is a lightweight, high-powered radio set having a normal range of from 200 to 2,000 miles. The SCR 284 for pack transport weighs over 100 pounds and has a normal range of 5 to 20 miles.

[11] The SCR 177–S operated very well in jungle but was extremely heavy to carry. It weighs about 700 pounds and has a range of 30 to 100 miles.

[12] The SCR 300 is a portable 32-pound set with an expected range of 5 miles.

tioned best only in the daytime when the signals of other stations were generally silent. The AN/PRC-1's required manpower, not always available, to crank their hand generators.

The operators, at first an inexperienced cross section of the services, learned to get the messages through. They often marched all day and then worked most of the night sending out and receiving communications or repairing their equipment. Upon the communications sections rested the responsibility for keeping channels open to coordinate the unit's operations with those of the main Chinese force, to requisition food and ammunition for the unit's existence in the enemy's jungle, and to call for air support at critical moments. All this they did effectively.

First Mission: Walawbum

B Y 24 FEBRUARY 1944 the Chinese 22d and 38th Divisions had driven 60 miles into the Hukawng Valley and were advancing southward against the Japanese 18th Division, which had about 7,000 men near and north of Maingkwan (Map No. 27, inside back cover). Strong jungle-hidden defensive positions, each manned by 40 to 100 Japanese, protected the Kamaing Road, the only motor route through the valley, the main supply artery for the enemy, and the key to control of the valley by either side. The Chinese forces were making their main drive along the axis of this road. The 112th and 113th Regiments of the 38th Division, having taken Taihpa Ga and cleared the area between the Tawang and Tanai Hka [13] (rivers) north of the road, were attacking south toward Maingkwan. Twenty miles to the west, beyond a 4,000-foot range of hills, the 65th Regiment of the 22d Division had captured Taro on 2 February and was working southeast in an advance that covered the right flank of the main effort.

On the Move

General Stilwell planned to coordinate the employment of the 5307th with the main operations in the Hukawng Valley by sending the Marauders on wide encircling movements east of the Chinese forces to establish road blocks behind the Japanese front lines (Map No. 6, page 33). For their first mission he ordered the Marauders to cut the Kamaing Road in the vicinity of Walawbum and to attack a

---

[13] Tanai is an alternate name for the Chindwin in this area.

forward command post believed to be near there. The Marauders were to move from Ningbyen to Tanja Ga and await General Stilwell's instructions to jump off. These instructions were to be given at the moment when Chinese operations along the road to the north of Maingkwan would most benefit by an attack in the rear of the Japanese lines.

To get into position for the jump-off, the 1st Battalion at 0600 on 24 February started over the trail from Ningbyen on a 5-day march to Tanja Ga. The 2d Battalion followed at 0900; the 3d at 1100. Each battalion moved out in column of combat teams, and the order of march afforded maximum protection. The I and R (Intelligence and Reconnaissance) Platoon was the point of the column and was followed by a rifle platoon. A rifle company, with half the heavy weapons platoon, was next in line. Combat team headquarters and the medical detachment, in the middle of the formation, preceded another rifle platoon and the rest of the heavy weapons.

In order to prevent surprise attacks, the I and R platoons scouted the trails in advance of the main elements of the combat teams and on the flanks. On the 25th the I and R Platoon of Orange Combat Team ran into an enemy patrol near Nzang Ga. In a sharp exchange of shots one Japanese was killed and one Marauder, Cpl. Warner Katz, was slightly wounded. On the same day, Pvt. Robert W. Landis, leading scout of Blue Combat Team's I and R Platoon, was killed by machine-gun fire as he approached Lanem Ga.

When the Marauders arrived in the vicinity of Tanja Ga on the afternoon of 28 February, they received orders from General Stilwell to proceed as quickly as possible to Walawbum. The steady advance of the Chinese on Maingkwan, forcing the enemy to retreat southward on the Kamaing Road, required the immediate employment of the 5307th. Coordinated with the Chinese operations, the Marauders' first mission was to hasten the enemy's withdrawal south of Walawbum by cutting his supply lines to forward troops.

Walawbum was 40 miles away; 3 days' march put the Marauders within striking distance. On 2 March, during a halt after the crossing of the Tanai River, General Merrill issued combat orders for this first mission (Insert on Map No. 6, page 33). Moving out at 1600, the 3d Battalion was to pass through Sabaw Ga and Lagang Ga and secure control of the Kamaing Road at Walawbum by seizing the

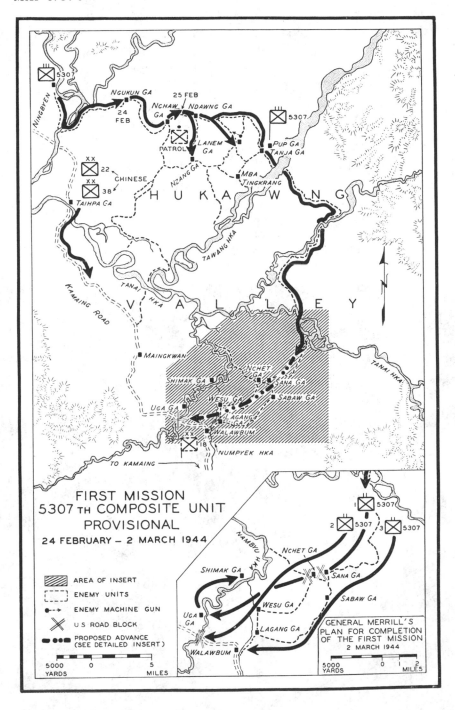

FIRST MISSION
5307 TH COMPOSITE UNIT
PROVISIONAL
24 FEBRUARY – 2 MARCH 1944

AREA OF INSERT
ENEMY UNITS
ENEMY MACHINE GUN
U S ROAD BLOCK
PROPOSED ADVANCE
(SEE DETAILED INSERT)

5000
YARDS   0   5
          MILES

GENERAL MERRILL'S
PLAN FOR COMPLETION
OF THE FIRST MISSION
2 MARCH 1944

5000
YARDS   0   1   2
          MILES

high ground along the Numpyek River east of the road. The 2d Battalion was to proceed via Wesu Ga, cut a trail through the jungle westerly to strike the Kamaing Road just east of the Nambyu River at a point 2½ miles west of Walawbum, and there construct and hold a road block. The 1st Battalion was to block the trails at Sana Ga and Nchet Ga, with a minimum of one platoon at each point. One combat team of the battalion was to establish combat patrols along the Nambyu River between Shimak Ga and Uga Ga. The rest of the battalion was to constitute a reserve at Wesu Ga. The Marauders were to hold their positions blocking the Kamaing Road until the Chinese, following up an enemy withdrawal, could occupy the area and relieve them.

ENTERING THE JUNGLE TRAIL, *the Marauder column is on the way to Walawbum.*

A VILLAGE BASHA *is searched by a lead scout as he passes through Tanja Ga.*

Kamaing Road Block

By dawn on 3 March all battalions of the 5307th had started for Walawbum, 15 miles away (Map No. 7, page 36). Until their presence was known by the Japanese in this rear area, about 20 miles behind the front lines, the Marauders met only small parties of the enemy moving to and from supply dumps, rear hospitals, or command posts established in and around the small villages near Walawbum. At Lagang Ga a group of seven, carrying one casualty, encountered members of the 3d Battalion Headquarters as they were passing through the village about noon. The headquarters section opened fire when the enemy party was 50 yards away and killed five Japanese before their machine gunner was able to fire effectively.

Orange Combat Team led the 3d Battalion and bivouacked for the night within a half mile of Walawbum, protected on its right flank by the I and R Platoon, under Lt. Logan E. Weston. During the afternoon Major Lew had sent Weston's platoon, relieved of acting as point of the column, across the Numpyek River. The platoon of

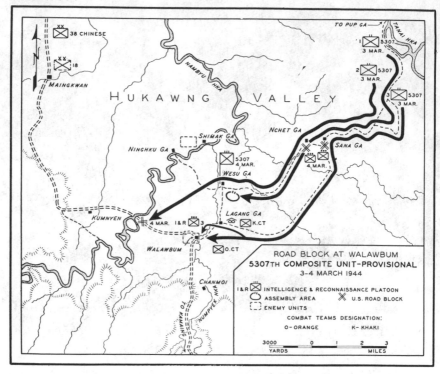

ROAD BLOCK AT WALAWBUM
5307TH COMPOSITE UNIT-PROVISIONAL
3-4 MARCH 1944

I & R ☒ INTELLIGENCE & RECONNAISSANCE PLATOON
◯ ASSEMBLY AREA   ☒ U.S. ROAD BLOCK
⌐⌐ ENEMY UNITS
COMBAT TEAMS DESIGNATION:
O- ORANGE   K- KHAKI

48 men with three automatic rifles dug in for the night on the west bank of the stream, a few hundred yards west of Orange Combat Team.

The night of 3 March found the 1st Battalion 2 miles east of Wesu Ga and the 2d Battalion in the same general area. All elements put out heavy local security, consisting of trail blocks and listening posts, and before morning many of these had tangled with small Japanese patrols and foraging parties. No casualties were suffered.

It seemed evident that the enemy had been confused by the sudden appearance of the 5307th in the Walawbum area. Early on 4 March the Japanese began to feel out the Marauder positions. At 0630 an enemy force of 30 vigorously attacked the Lagang Ga air strip, which Khaki Combat Team had constructed and had since been protecting for L-4 and L-5 liaison planes. The enemy arrived just as the Marauders were preparing their breakfast. Conditions of fog, as well as concealment offered by heavy brush and gullies, facilitated the enemy's approach. Nevertheless, a squad of riflemen, two light machine gunners, and 60-mm mortar men quickly drove off the force after 10 of its number had been killed. Six men from Khaki Combat Team were wounded during the engagement, and four of these were evacuated by liaison plane from the strip.

Within another hour a Japanese force of 90, coming from the direction of Walawbum, threatened Orange Combat Team's I and R Platoon in the heaviest fighting of the day (Map No. 8, below). Lieutenant Weston had moved his unit to higher ground along the river about 300 yards southwest of the position he had occupied during the night. On this higher ground he could stop any attempted enemy crossing of the river either up or down stream toward the flank of Orange Combat Team. At 0720 the platoon brushed with an enemy patrol on the west side of the river and shortly afterward met resistance from a Japanese group to the north. A little later another enemy group came at the platoon's position from the northwest, and a fourth and a fifth group advanced on it from the north and northeast.

MAP NO. 8

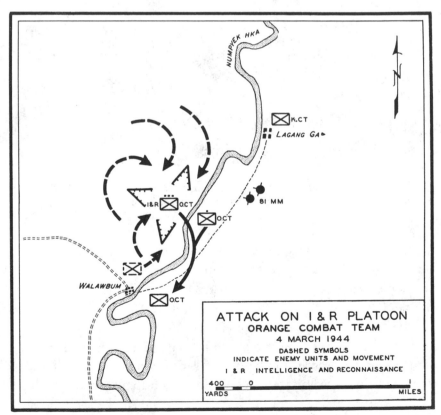

ATTACK ON I & R PLATOON
ORANGE COMBAT TEAM
4 MARCH 1944
DASHED SYMBOLS
INDICATE ENEMY UNITS AND MOVEMENT
I & R   INTELLIGENCE AND RECONNAISSANCE

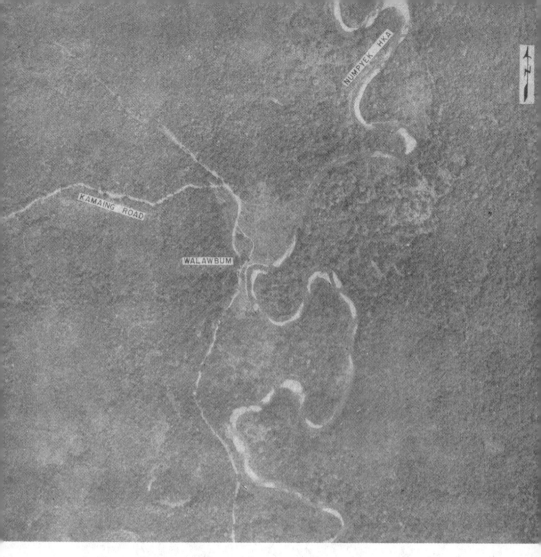

Labels on image: NUMPYEK HKA, KAMAING ROAD, WALAWBUM, N

WALAWBUM, *objective of the first mission, is a clearing in the thick jungle growth of the Hukawng Valley. (Aerial photograph from 11,000 feet.)*

Japanese officers were heard shouting orders to their men for these movements. Sgt. Henry H. Gosho, Nisei interpreter with Weston's platoon, was able to translate this information in time for shifting automatic weapons to meet each attack successfully. Nevertheless, mortar fire began to come very close, and by 1100 the platoon was pressed on three sides by superior enemy forces.

When the fourth enemy group was turned back, Lieutenant Weston signaled Major Lew by radio and asked for mortar fire from his 81-mm section. During and after the enemy's fifth attack, Lt. William E. Woomer fired 235 rounds of light, heavy, and smoke shells according to Lieutenant Weston's radioed directions. Under cover of mortar fire, the I and R Platoon waded the stream, carrying three litters. The Japanese attempted to follow but a squad from the team, forming a skirmish line, protected the crossing and stopped the enemy with heavy small-arms fire. The I and R Platoon, having held up a strong enemy attack on Orange Combat Team's right flank until it reached its objective, withdrew to the southwest and dug in with the team. The platoon and the mortar section had destroyed two-thirds of the Japanese attacking force, estimated at 90 men.

Orange Combat Team established a perimeter along the Numpyek River on the high ground facing Walawbum and was in position to block the Kamaing Road with mortars and machine guns (Map No. 7, page 36). In the afternoon Major Lew's men threw about 100 shells into the village and on the road. The Japanese replied with some mortar and artillery fire. The mortar shells landed around the perimeter, but the artillery ranged over it to Lagang Ga, where planes were dropping supplies to Khaki Combat Team. Neither Khaki nor Orange Combat Team suffered casualties from this enemy fire.

North of Walawbum two Japanese soldiers infiltrated the Marauder lines and almost succeeded in reaching General Merrill's command post, established temporarily at Wesu Ga. When they were discovered one was setting up a machine gun with which he could have wiped out the entire command group. The other was found worming his way through the heavy growth surrounding the headquarters. Both Japanese escaped, but a pool of blood on the ground showed that at least one was wounded.

Northwest of Walawbum the men of the 2d Battalion had been chopping their way through the jungle toward the Kamaing Road. Meeting no serious resistance, they reached the road at dusk, constructed a block and a perimeter defense, and dug in for the night.

The 18th Division's telephone communications from the front to headquarters at Kamaing ran along the road and so passed through the perimeter of the road block established by the 2d Battalion. Tec. 4 Roy H. Matsumoto, a Nisei assigned to the 2d Battalion for intelligence operations, tapped the enemy's telephone line. One of the conversations he heard concerned the troubles of a Japanese sergeant in charge of an ammunition dump. The sergeant had with him only three soldiers armed with rifles and begged "help and advice" from his commanding officer because he had learned of the 2d Battalion's arrival at the road. The sergeant, in reporting the location of the 2d Battalion, gave away his own position. When American planes appeared for a supply drop, the 2d Battalion signaled the crews to send back to the enemy dump fighters or bombers with "help and advice" of an unexpected kind.

On 4 March, while guarding the rear of the 2d and 3d Battalions, two platoons of the 1st Battalion had established blocks near Sana Ga and Nchet Ga on the trails leading into Walawbum. Their patrols inflicted heavy casualties on unwary small parties of the enemy, but nothing approaching a large engagement materialized in that section. From Wesu Ga, where most of the 1st Battalion was in reserve, Red and White Combat Teams sent out strong reconnaissance groups to the air strip at Lagang Ga and across the Nambyu River to Ninghku Ga. Red Combat Team's patrol met no resistance. White's patrol ran into a group of Japanese near Ninghku Ga. The Marauders killed two of the group and dispersed the rest, averting another possible attack on the 5307th's command post.

Japanese Withdrawal

On March 5 the Japanese made several efforts to dislodge the forces blocking their supply road (Map No. 9, page 41). The 2d Battalion underwent considerable shelling and turned back six infantry attacks, at a cost of one man killed and five wounded. South of Walawbum, after heavy mortar fire and some 77-mm artillery shelling, strong Japanese patrols moved toward Orange Combat Team with the evident intention of finding its flanks. Anticipating just such moves, Major Lew had prepared ambush positions along the east bank of the Numpyek River, and Orange Combat Team took heavy toll of the enemy as they were crossing the stream. Seventy-five Japanese dead were counted; Orange lost one killed and seven wounded. Toward evening all activity against the 2d and 3d Battalions slackened, but enemy reinforcements were on their way from Kamaing. Strafed and bombed by our planes en route, they nevertheless kept coming; the noisy slamming of tail gates after dark indicated that truck after truck was arriving and discharging its cargo of reinforcements.

Messages intercepted on the telephone-tap by the 2d Battalion

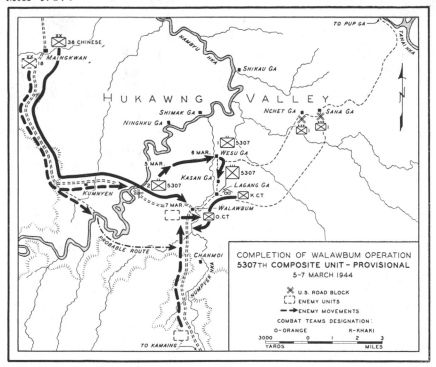

COMPLETION OF WALAWBUM OPERATION
5307TH COMPOSITE UNIT - PROVISIONAL
5-7 MARCH 1944

※ U.S. ROAD BLOCK
[_] ENEMY UNITS
➤ ENEMY MOVEMENTS
COMBAT TEAMS DESIGNATION:
O-ORANGE   K-KHAKI

proved that the Japanese were still confused by the American activities. Finally, Matsumoto reported that forward elements of the Japanese 18th Division had been ordered to withdraw from the Maingkwan area, crossing the Nambyu River south of Kumnyen. To screen the withdrawal of the main units, which were apparently not intending to use the Kamaing Road, the enemy was planning to attack the 2d Battalion at 2300 that night. The Japanese had artillery available for this attack, and the 2d Battalion, with only a limited amount of mortar and machine-gun ammunition, was in no condition to stop them from pushing through the road block. The battalion had fought for 36 hours without food or water. Colonel McGee explained the situation to General Merrill by phone. The General advised the 2d Battalion to withdraw after dark toward Wesu Ga and join the 3d Battalion east of the Numpyek River. The Marauders blocked the road with trees, placed booby traps in the area, and withdrew along the trail they had cut 2 days before. Fortunately, they themselves were alert to the danger of booby traps and drove a mule ahead of them. The mule was blown to bits. Arriving at Wesu Ga by noon the following day,

41

6 March, Colonel McGee and his men picked up an air drop of rations and ammunition, filled their canteens, and hurried toward Lagang Ga where they could support the 3d Battalion if they were needed.

After the 2d Battalion vacated its road-block position west of Walawbum on the night of 5 March, Orange Combat Team was holding the only position still commanding the Kamaing Road. Khaki Combat Team was withdrawn from the Lagang Ga air strip early on the morning of 6 March and moved out to strengthen Major Lew's position by advancing beyond his left flank to a point where the Numpyek River makes a sharp U bend. General Merrill also moved 4 miles nearer the position of the 3d Battalion, changing his command post from Wesu Ga to Lagang Ga.

From dawn the Japanese, in what was presumably a further effort to cover the withdrawal of their main force, poured a steady stream of mortar fire on Orange Combat Team and about midmorning supplemented the mortar fire by medium artillery. Major Lew's men, now standing the brunt of the whole attack, were well protected in fox holes roofed with logs and managed to keep the upper hand throughout the day.

Elements of the combat team disrupted the enemy's plans to organize an attacking force to the south. Sgt. Andrew B. Pung directed mortar fire from the 81-mm section on a concentration area for troops arriving from Kamaing. Perched in a tree 30 feet from the ground, he secured several direct hits, one of the shells landing in the bed of a truck from which reinforcements were being unloaded. As a result of this accurate fire, no assaults materialized from the south.

Equal success was obtained against enemy efforts from the west. At 1715 two enemy companies, following each other in line of skirmishers and strongly supported by heavy machine-gun, mortar, and 77-mm fire, attempted to cross the river to attack Orange Combat Team's position. Except for mortars, the Marauders held their fire until the enemy reached the western river bank, some 25 yards away. Then they let loose with their automatic weapons and tore great gaps in the Japanese line. Two heavy machine guns, placed on the river bank with clear fields of fire, used 5,000 rounds each with deadly effect. The attack wilted, and 400 Japanese lay dead on the open ground near the river.

By now Orange Combat Team's ammunition was low. Khaki

Combat Team, which was still moving to get into position south of Orange, rushed up five mule loads of mortar shells and machine-gun cartridges. But before the ammunition arrived the Japanese had retired. The only casualties Orange Combat Team suffered were three slightly wounded. During the hour of combat the Japanese put in a great deal of small-arms fire, but they were aiming uphill and most of the fire passed overhead.

Mission Accomplished

At Kasan Ga, more than an hour before the last Japanese attack at 1715, General Merrill met a Chinese battalion commander who had just arrived, ahead of his regiment, to arrange relief of the Marauders at Walawbum. General Merrill's present intelligence estimates indicated that the enemy was bringing in reinforcements from the south to make a stand at Walawbum. He therefore decided to disengage the Marauders, pull back, circle around to the east, and cut the Kamaing road near Chanmoi, again maneuvering his forces to the rear of the Japanese. The Chinese regiment would take over the Marauder positions at Walawbum.

However, before General Merrill's orders for this move could be executed, the situation at Walawbum had changed. The Japanese had suddenly retired toward Kamaing after their costly attack on Orange Combat Team. Also, the Chinese 22d and 38th Divisions had captured Maingkwan and were pushing rapidly to the south in pursuit of the main enemy force retreating toward Chanmoi on a road which bypassed the Marauder position. Further American efforts were unnecessary.

The 38th Division arrived in the Walawbum area on 7 March. The Chinese made contact with the Marauders so quickly and unexpectedly that the first encounter resulted in an exchange of shots. The Chinese, failing to recognize the American helmets, fired on Red Combat Team disposed along the river east of Wesu Ga. The Marauders replied with rifle and mortar fire, and shooting continued until a Chinese interpreter identified the opposing force. The Americans quickly waded across the stream to find a major and three enlisted men badly wounded. Marauder doctors rushed to the scene, and men from Red Combat Team carried the injured Chinese to the air strip for evacuation.

Shortly after this incident, the Chinese 38th Division entered

TROOPS OF THE CHINESE 38th DIVISION *arrive at Walawbum, marking an end of the first mission. The Marauders on the left withdraw up the trail as the Chinese take over positions in the town.*

Walawbum with almost no opposition. At 1845 that evening General Merrill held a staff meeting to inform the assembled officers that the first phase of the Marauder operation had ended. He conveyed to the group General Stilwell's congratulations for a job well done and requested the officers to relay the message to their men. A 3-day rest period, he announced, was now in order.

During the rest period the men of the 5307th cleaned and overhauled their equipment and made repairs and replacements wherever necessary. The Americans and nearby Chinese troops set up a joint perimeter around Sana Ga and Shikau Ga. The two groups exchanged rations, battle souvenirs, and money and went swimming together. Morale was superb.

In 5 days, from the jump-off on 3 March to the fall of Walawbum on 7 March, the Americans had killed 800 of the enemy, had cooperated with the Chinese to force a major Japanese withdrawal, and had paved the way for further Allied progress. This was accomplished at a cost to the Marauders of 8 men killed and 37 wounded. Up to this point 19 patients had been evacuated with malaria, 8 with other fevers (mostly dengue), 10 with psychoneurosis, and 33 with injuries. Miscellaneous sicknesses totaled 109. Of the 2,750 men who started toward Walawbum, about 2,500 remained to carry on.

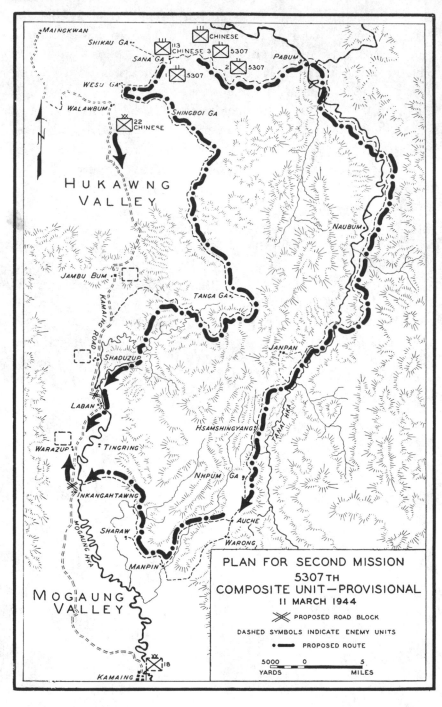

PLAN FOR SECOND MISSION
5307TH
COMPOSITE UNIT—PROVISIONAL
11 MARCH 1944

PROPOSED ROAD BLOCK

DASHED SYMBOLS INDICATE ENEMY UNITS

PROPOSED ROUTE

5000   0   5
YARDS   MILES

Second Mission: Shaduzup and Inkangahtawng

THE ADVANCE TO Walawbum gave General Stilwell control of the Hukawng Valley (Map. No. 27, inside back cover). The next phase of the offensive would center on the corridor formed by the Mogaung Valley. The entrance to this corridor lies over the low hills near Jambu Bum that serve as a watershed between the tributaries of the Hukawng and Mogaung. Spearheading the main advance, the Chinese 22d Division was crowding the Japanese southward along the Kamaing Road toward Jambu Bum. Twenty-five miles to the west, the Chinese 65th Regiment was still covering the right flank in a push toward Tasu Bum. Once again General Stilwell planned to use the Marauders on an encircling mission east of the Kamaing Road. Penetrating 15 and 20 miles to the rear of the main Japanese forces, two Marauder columns were to cut enemy supply lines and communications and harass rear areas.

On 11 March, the day after he had received General Stilwell's plan for this operation, General Merrill held a staff meeting to brief his officers on the mission (Map No. 10, page 46). Marauder columns were to strike simultaneously at two points along the Kamaing Road and establish road blocks, to pinch out hostile elements between these blocks, and then to attack north or south along the road or in both directions, as the situation warranted. To insure maximum freedom of action for the Marauders, two regiments of the Chinese 38th Division were to take part in the operation. Following the Marauder units, these Chinese troops were to take over the blocks as soon as they

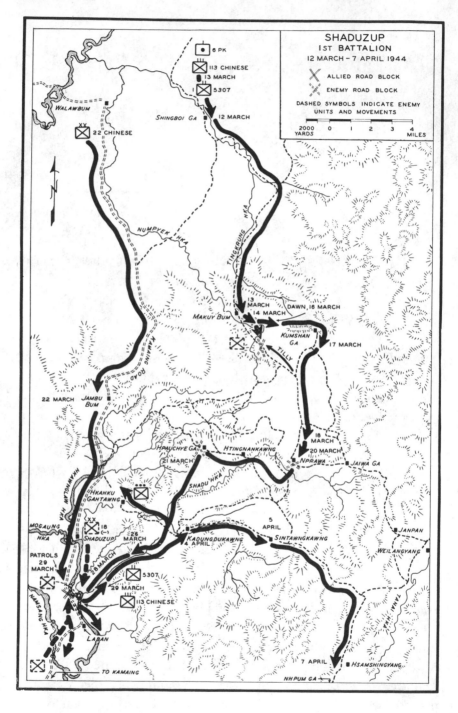

had been established, enabling the Marauders to exploit the situation as it developed.

The 1st Battalion, followed by a Chinese regiment, was to proceed from Sana Ga in a flanking movement to cut the Kamaing Road near Shaduzup. On the 50-mile hike to Shaduzup the battalion was to follow a trail running through the southeastern end of the Hukawng Valley and along the southwestern slopes of the Kumon Range to the Mogaung Valley. The 2d and 3d Battalions, also followed by a Chinese regiment, were to make a wider sweep of about 80 miles to block the Kamaing Road at Inkangahtawng, south of the Shaduzup block. Their trail followed the Tanai River in a constricted valley between two main chains of the Kumon Mountains; beyond Janpan, the trail wound up the side of the valley and led over a series of razor-backed ridges, with differences of elevation amounting to as much as 1,600 feet in 4 miles. Beyond Auche, the column would reach the Mogaung watershed and strike west to the road. The Marauder parties were to take about 2 weeks getting to their positions on the road.

On the Move to Shaduzup

At 0700 on 12 March the 1st Battalion started for Shaduzup; the Chinese 113th Regiment and 6th Pack Artillery Battery followed (Map No. 11, page 48). In the next 2 days the 1st Battalion covered about 20 miles to Makuy Bum, always watching for enemy patrols along the trails. From this point on, the Marauders were in rough hills as high as 2,000 feet, and the difficulties of progress were increased by the tendency of trails to avoid the stream beds and to take the hills as they came.

On the 14th the I and R Platoon of White Combat Team, feeling out the trail south of Makuy Bum several miles in advance of the main column, made the first encounter with enemy forces. Warned by finding footprints, the men of the platoon, commanded by Lt. Samuel V. Wilson, redoubled their caution and slipped up unobserved on a group of Japanese sitting around camp fires just off the narrow jungle path. The Marauders' surprise fire killed four Japanese and one Burman but stirred up a veritable hornet's nest. The enemy proved to be 150 strong, and the platoon quickly dispersed into the jungle. Withdrawing up the trail, one of the Marauders encountered Lt. William C. Evans, commander of Red Combat Team's I and R

Platoon. Upon hearing the plight of Lieutenant Wilson's men, Lieutenant Evans sent a report of the situation back to the main column and hastened with his unit to assist in clearing the trail.

A rifle platoon from the main column under Lt. John P. McElmurry also rushed forward to help Lieutenant Wilson, and the three platoons drove the Japanese across the nearby Numpyek River. Following them closely, Lieutenant McElmurry's riflemen seized commanding ground on the far side of the river, held this bridgehead against an enemy attack, and covered the crossing of the main Marauder force.

This engagement had disclosed the forward movement of the Marauders. On the following day, 15 March, they had to fight eight separate skirmishes with small parties during the first 1½ miles' advance. Lieutenant Evans' platoon, leading the battalion column, bore the brunt of the enemy assaults. In the next half mile the Marauders met a larger group of Japanese, apparently the same one that Lieutenant Wilson had encountered the night before. This group was armed with both light and heavy machine guns; for the first time the Marauders encountered use of the enemy's S-shaped machine-gun formation to block a trail (Sketch No. 1, page 51). The Japanese pinned down the lead squad with machine-gun fire and then threw mortar shells behind the squad so fast that it could not be easily supported by the rest of the platoon. Every time the Marauders got mortars into action against the Japanese machine guns and made an enveloping movement through the thick growth beside the trail, the enemy displaced 100 to 150 yards down the trail and repeated his delaying tactics. Maneuver in this section of the jungle was hampered by growth so dense that, once off the trail, men could easily get lost within 10 feet of each other.

Though the Marauders were unaware of the fact, they were receiving considerable assistance in their battle. A group of irregular Kachin guerrillas, led by Lt. James L. Tilly (Detachment 101, Office of Strategic Services) [14] was ambushing and harassing the rear of the Japanese forces. The Kachin operations kept the enemy group "bouncing" from east to west to meet attacks and increased the enemy casualties. Unfortunately, Colonel Osborne had no information about the Kachin activities. In view of the determined resistance the

[14] Detachment 101, Office of Strategic Services, was operating in Burma to recruit, equip, train, and lead Kachin guerrillas. General Stilwell reinforced General Merrill's command with these OSS-led native groups. They gathered military intelligence, furnished information about roads and trails, and worked ahead of and with the Marauders during much of their campaign.

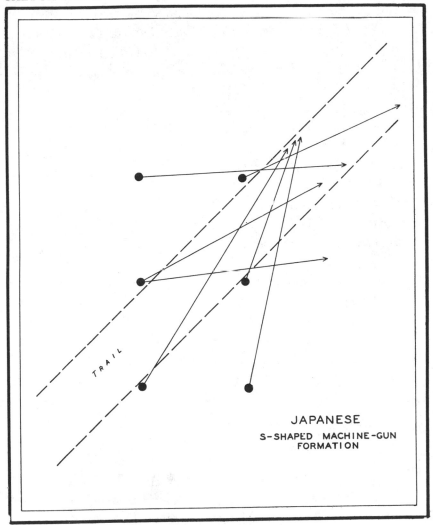

JAPANESE

S-SHAPED MACHINE-GUN
FORMATION

TRAIL

Marauder column was meeting, he could only foresee delays which would prevent his reaching the Kamaing Road on schedule and prevent coordination of his efforts with those of the other Marauder group. Therefore, he decided to cut a trail around the Japanese force.

Leaving Red Combat Team to keep the Japanese occupied, Colonel Osborne pulled White Combat Team back a short distance. It was late evening and little could be accomplished in the darkness. But at dawn on 16 March White Combat Team started chopping a path through the jungle toward Kumshan Ga. Red Combat Team kept in contact with the enemy until late that afternoon, then pulled back and—together with the Chinese 113th Regiment which had caught up with the team during the day—followed the trail cut by White Combat Team. Every member of White Combat Team, including officers, took turns at the arduous task of hewing and chopping through the jungle. But it took 2 days of back-breaking labor with kukris and machetes to reach Kumshan Ga, a distance of only 4 miles. Clumps of bamboo were sometimes too large to be detoured, and growth was so densely interwoven that the stems could not fall when lopped off at ground level. They had to be cut again some 6 feet above the ground, turning the trail into a sort of tunnel.

When the 1st Battalion reached Kumshan Ga on the afternoon of 17 March supplies were needed. While the request for an air drop was going back to the Dinjan base, the Marauders picked the best available spot in the mountainous area and cleared it for a dropping field. However, in locating this field the transports had consumed so much time that their gasoline supply was dangerously low. The pilots, therefore, advised the Marauders that they would make the drop next morning and returned to base. The Marauders improved the field, and when the planes returned the following day the drop was made. Because of hills encircling the drop ground, the transports had to unload from a high altitude and much of the free-dropped grain was lost. Some of the parachutes floated over a nearby hill, but all were searched out and their loads secured.

As soon as the supplies were packed, the 1st Battalion pushed forward vigorously over the trail leading south and by nightfall of 18 March had reached a point 2 miles northwest of Jaiwa Ga. Here it made contact with the 50 Kachins under Lieutenant Tilly, who provided guides for the rest of the march to Shaduzup.

The next point of enemy resistance was reached on 20 March, when the battalion entered Nprawa. As the lead scouts were plodding along the trail their Kachin guides suddenly became talkative. Having no interpreter handy, the Marauders nonchalantly ascribed the natives' "jabbering" to a desire for food or cigarettes and provided the Kachins with both. Actually, the Kachins had announced that a Nambu (Japanese machine gun) position lay directly ahead, and they assumed that the food and cigarettes were rewards for this information. The machine gun soon disclosed itself, killing one Marauder and wounding two. Luckily, the Japanese were impetuous in opening fire on the

KACHIN GUIDES *lead the Marauders cross-country along uncharted footpaths.*

scouts; had they waited, more men would have been caught in their field of fire. In an hour the 1st Battalion's mortar fire forced the enemy to withdraw. This incident taught the Marauders a lesson; thereafter, native remarks were always interpreted.

On 21 March the 1st Battalion stopped to pick up a 5-day supply drop in a rice paddy near Htingnankawng, and Red Combat Team, in the lead, reached Hpauchye Ga. After clearing this village, only five miles east of the Kamaing Road, the battalion discovered that every trail was blocked or ambushed. The advance platoon of Red Combat Team, commanded by Lt. Harry B. Coburn, ran into an ambush and at first tried to push through or bypass the enemy positions. As the platoon was cutting a trail around a trail block, the scouts sighted a Japanese group lounging beside well-made fox holes. The Marauders crept forward cautiously and opened fire, killing seven Japanese. When Coburn's men took over the fox holes for a brief rest, the enemy returned in greater force and attacked them. The fox holes were so well located that the Marauders were able to break up the attack quickly, inflicting additional casualties on the enemy. However, further reconnaissance revealed no trail open to the Kamaing Road. In order to preserve an element of surprise for the establishment of the block near Shaduzup, Colonel Osborne considered it highly important for the 1st Battalion to have as little contact with the enemy as possible. Therefore, he again decided to leave the well-guarded trails and to cut a path southward, cross country, from Hpauchye Ga toward the Chengun River.

During the next 2 days, 23 and 24 March, the going was strenuous and difficult. Time and again the men gained passage through the almost impenetrable growth only by slowly hacking out a path. Frequently they had to unload the animals and carry the supplies by hand up steep hillsides. Colonel Osborne was successful, however, in maintaining secrecy of movement, for during the hike of 5 miles cross country the Marauders met no Japanese.

Into Position

From Lieutenant Tilly, Colonel Osborne had learned that the enemy held Shaduzup in some strength (Map No. 11, page 48). Three hundred Japanese were estimated to be there and five to six hundred more in the vicinity of Jambu Bum to the north. In order to deceive the enemy and avoid being attacked by a combined enemy force, Colonel Osborne decided upon sending one platoon to make a feint toward Shaduzup from the northeast. The main battalion column was to proceed down the Chengun River to the Kamaing Road.

Following Colonel Osborne's decision, Lieutenant McElmurry led one rifle platoon along a trail running northwest to Hkahku Gahtawng. Just before entering this village the platoon surprised two enemy soldiers, evidently a reconnaissance party, carrying only maps and sketching equipment. Both of these men dropped as the Marauders fired, but a moment later one of them leaped to his feet and disappeared into the underbrush. McElmurry passed on through Hkahku Gahtawng. The village soon afterward became a mortar target for the Japanese, who continued to throw shells at it throughout the night. This feint to the north undoubtedly contributed to the complete surprise achieved the next day by the 1st Battalion's arrival to the south of Shaduzup.

Colonel Osborne had decided to place his road block where the Mogaung River makes a U bend at its confluence with the Chengun River. At this location, approximately 4 miles south of Shaduzup, the river runs parallel to the road. On the night of 26 March the 1st Battalion bivouacked by the upper reaches of the Chengun River. Next day the Marauders, often wading downstream to avoid cutting trails, made their way south to within a mile of their objective.

The I and R Platoon of White Combat Team reported Japanese present, apparently in large numbers, some bathing in the Mogaung River and others grenading fish. There appeared to be an enemy camp between the Mogaung River and the Kamaing Road. Further scouting revealed that at least one Japanese company was installed in this camp and that there was another and larger camp a short distance to the south. The enemy had quantities of food and clothing stored in bashas or under canvas covers.

Colonel Osborne was still confident that the Japanese were unaware of the Marauders' presence, for even the advance platoon had not been discovered. He therefore planned a surprise night attack, to begin early on 28 March. He selected three points for crossing the Mogaung River and organized the battalion into six columns for the attack on the northern Japanese camp. Three columns were to converge upon the camp. Three others, closely following the first three, were to be sent either to add impetus to the shock, wherever resistance might be met, or to fill any gap that might develop in the lines. The second three columns could also, if necessary, be used for flanking operations or to meet any supporting enemy force that might be rushed up from the southern Japanese camp.

Major Johnson's White Combat Team formed the three columns making the first attack. At 0300 the team started out in complete silence and cautiously waded the Mogaung River. Red Combat Team took position on the east bank to cover the south flank of the attacking force. The Chinese 113th Regiment was in reserve.

The Japanese were caught completely by surprise. Not one sentry was encountered as White Combat Team's three columns crept into position. Dawn broke. Small fires began to crackle in the unsuspecting Japanese camp as early risers started to prepare breakfast.

Suddenly the attack order was given by radio. With fixed bayonets the Marauders swept through the camp. Naked or half-dressed, the panic-stricken Japanese scattered in all directions. Those with weapons fired wild, ineffectual shots. Many of them were killed or wounded by bayonets, grenades, and tommy guns.

The platoon led by Lt. Meredith Caldwell, Jr., was the first to reach the Kamaing Road, and his men immediately dug a protective perimeter which constituted the road block. When the perimeter was finished, the men changed into clean underwear which they had found in a captured enemy truck and devoured the rice and fish that had been left cooking over the enemy's breakfast fires.

The Marauders expected a counterattack; it was not long in coming. By 0700 Japanese snipers were very active, and further digging in, although not discontinued, became difficult. By 0900 Japanese artillery opened up on Red Combat Team on the east bank of the river.

Preliminary reconnaissance parties had not discovered that the enemy had artillery. White Combat Team's perimeter was so close to the rise in ground behind which the enemy gun positions were located that for the time being the Marauders were masked and not a vulnerable target. By 1000, however, the Japanese managed to get another battery from farther north ranged in, and soon 77- and 150-mm shells came pouring down on the perimeter.

The stab by the 1st Battalion at the rear of the Japanese seriously diverted their attention from the Chinese 22d Division advancing down the road from Walawbum. After several concerted attacks, the Chinese had reached Jambu Bum, at the threshold of the Mogaung Valley, a few days before the Marauders established their road block below Shaduzup, 10 miles to the south. Enemy troops were hurriedly pulled back along the road to help cope with this new threat to their rear, thus permitting the Chinese to make more rapid progress against slackening Japanese resistance.

Caught between these Allied forces, the Japanese made determined efforts to extricate themselves. By midday White Combat Team's perimeter had undergone an attack from the north which was turned back with heavy losses to the enemy. At 1300 another attack, supported by artillery, developed from the west, and reinforcements were arriving in trucks from the south. But by this time the Marauders had an excellent final protective line which the Japanese were unable to penetrate. All that afternoon the enemy attacked in varying strength, nearly always from a different quarter, and each time the Marauders repulsed them after inflicting heavy casualties.

Lieutenant McElmurry and Lt. Charles R. Scott crouched together in a fox hole during one of the attacks. McElmurry called Scott's attention to a Japanese officer who appeared on the road. But Scott had also seen the officer and shot him while McElmurry was drawing a bead. In the next half hour 12 Japanese were killed as they attempted to retrieve their officer's body.

The assaults tapered off in late afternoon, but all that night enemy artillery pounded both the road block and Red Combat Team's position across the river. Since the Marauders had no artillery, they used their mortars and threw grenades whenever they heard a suspicious sound along their front.

The 1st Battalion is Relieved

The Marauders had established themselves firmly. Following the plan of operations, the Chinese 113th Regiment moved in just before dawn of 29 March and took over both the road-block perimeter and the supporting positions to the east of the river (Map No. 11, page 48). When the Chinese opened up with their pack artillery, the enemy guns quieted down. By 1000 the 1st Battalion had withdrawn about a mile up the Chengun River to a Seagrave [15] hospital unit which had been set up during the last 2 days. The weary Marauders rested, listening to opposing Chinese and Japanese artillery fire from just over the hill. The action on the Kamaing Road had cost the 1st Battalion 8 men killed and 35 wounded.

By 29 March the Japanese had lost more than 300 men south of Shaduzup, and during the day they withdrew toward Kamaing. One battalion of the Chinese 113th Regiment followed the retreating enemy as far as Laban, approximately a mile to the south. At 1500 patrols from this Chinese battalion met patrols from the Chinese 22d Division pushing down through the Hukawng-Mogaung corridor and the Kamaing Road was declared open to Laban.

General Merrill's instructions to Colonel Osborne had been to

---

[15] Col. Gordon S. Seagrave, an American medical missionary in Burma for 20 years, had furnished mobile hospital units to General Stilwell's Chinese armies in 1942. He had continued to serve them at the Ramgarh Training Center after their withdrawal from Burma and had followed the Chinese 22d and 38th Divisions back into Burma during the 1943–1944 offensive.

rejoin the rest of the 5307th Composite Unit, which would probably be near Hsamshingyang, as soon as practicable after accomplishing his mission. This order was confirmed when the 1st Battalion received a message to proceed to Janpan by easy stages.

The shortest route for the 1st Battalion from Shaduzup to Janpan was directly across the western chain of hills in the Kumon Range to the Tanai Valley. Movement was started on 30 March. The trail became increasingly rugged as the men backtracked along the Chengun River and headed for the ridges rising east of the corridor to 2,000, 3,000, and almost 4,000 feet. In a day's march of 10 hours they sometimes covered little more than a mile.

A SEAGRAVE HOSPITAL UNIT *treats a wounded soldier. A native nurse gives the patient ether by the drop method.*

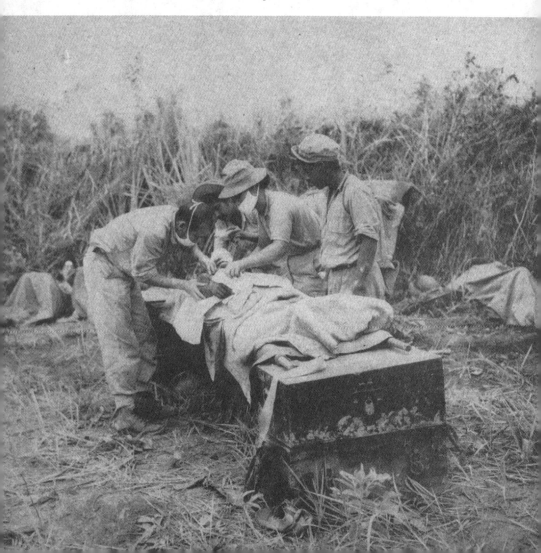

From 1 to 3 April the 1st Battalion was out of contact with head-quarters. A sack of grain, falling from a supply plane during an air drop, had crashed into the unit's only long-range radio, putting it out of operation. On the 3d, Colonel Osborne was unwilling to wait any longer to hear from General Merrill and returned to Shaduzup, where the Chinese headquarters had a radio net with the Marauder head-quarters. While Colonel Osborne was gone, the battalion's radio operator succeeded in repairing his machine, and simultaneously the Chinese and battalion radios picked up an urgent message from the General directing that the 1st Battalion make all haste to Hsamshingyang.

On the Move to Inkangahtawng

While the 1st Battalion was operating with great success in the Shaduzup area, the 2d and 3d Battalions were carrying out their part of the two-column mission (Map No. 12, page 60). According to plan they were to block the Kamaing Road near Inkangahtawng in the Mogaung Valley. This would cut the enemy's supply artery almost halfway between the Japanese 18th Division's front lines north of the Hukawng-Mogaung corridor and the division's base at Kamaing. Timed to coincide with the strike at Shaduzup, 10 miles to the north, the Inkangahtawng block would increase the threat to the enemy's rear and add to the difficulties of his retirement.

At 0700 on 12 March, the 2d Battalion pulled out of Shikau Ga and Wesu Ga and hit the trail for Pabum. At 0800 the command group followed, and the 3d Battalion, bringing up the rear of the column, got under way at 1000. The Chinese regiment scheduled to accompany this column was not finally available to follow the Marauder battalions.

During the first 3 days, 12–14 March, the Marauders stopped their advance only long enough to pick up an air drop. At Pabum they headed south along the Tanai River, and on 15 March they reached Naubum where their route was approaching the hills. In this village the column was met by Capt. Vincent L. Curl, another member of Detachment 101, with a force of Kachin guerrillas. This group of approximately 300 natives, armed with everything from flintlocks to captured Japanese weapons, joined the Marauders.

On 16 March the 2d and 3d Battalions crossed about 15 miles of rough, muddy trail to Weilangyang. The Kachins warned the Americans that the Japanese were now near, so patrols were sent out along all routes in the vicinity, and blocks and ambushes were established to the northwest and south.

At Weilangyang General Merrill stopped the 2d and 3d Battalions to wait for definite instructions covering their movement toward Inkangahtawng and to receive a food drop. During their 2-day halt the men rested, washed their clothes, and fished and swam in the river. They cleared a field where supply planes dropped the large quantity of food scheduled to arrive. Elephants, which Captain Curl

MAP NO. 12

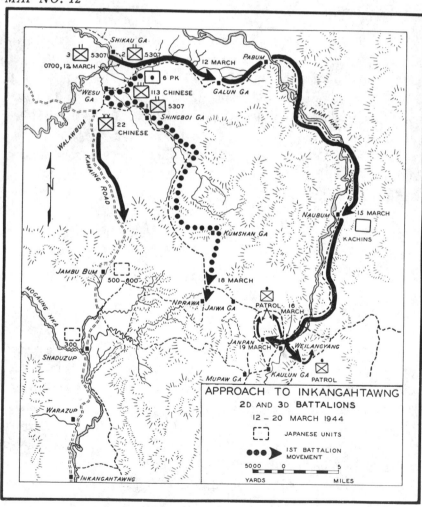

APPROACH TO INKANGAHTAWNG
2D AND 3D BATTALIONS
12 - 20 MARCH 1944

JAPANESE UNITS

1ST BATTALION MOVEMENT

NATIVE BRIDGE ACROSS THE TANAI RIVER *south of Naubum is used by men of the 2d and 3d Battalions en route to Inkangahtawng. Horses and mules ford the four-foot deep stream.*

had "borrowed" from the Japanese, who in turn had "borrowed" them from the Kachins, carried the packages to a distributing area. Capt. James W. Parker, the unit dental officer, came in by plane and started work on all those whose teeth urgently needed attention. With him he brought dispatches which gave General Merrill last-minute reports on enemy activity and an account of what was happening to the 1st Battalion, then north of Nprawa.

Just at dusk on 18 March a liaison plane dropped a message from General Stilwell, instructing the 2d and 3d Battalions to protect the flank of the Chinese advance by blocking approaches along the Tanai River from the south. General Merrill had expected this order and decided to move southward to Kaulun Ga and Mupaw Ga. At Kaulun Ga he would command the trails on both banks of the river, and at Mupaw Ga, on the highest hill in the area, he would have observation along the trail 2 miles west of the river.

At 1300 on 19 March the 2d Battalion, together with the command group, moved out to Janpan on the way to Kaulun Ga and Mupaw Ga, leaving the 3d Battalion to follow shortly. Captain Curl and his Kachin guerrillas went along with the 2d Battalion.

At 1030 on the following day, General Merrill received radio orders from General Stilwell directing the 2d and 3d Battalions to accomplish their original mission as well as to block any Japanese movement along the Tanai River. He estimated that an enemy force of about 2,000 was south and west of Kamaing.

General Merrill's orders dividing the Marauders' efforts included the following provisions for movement (Map No. 13, page 64):

"The 2d Battalion and the Khaki Combat Team of the 3d Battalion under command of Col. Charles N. Hunter will move south on the [trail to] Warong . . ., reconnoiter the trails south toward Kamaing, and move rapidly to seize and hold . . . a block on the main road between Warazup and Malakawng in the general vicinity of Inkangahtawng.

"Orange Combat Team will remain in the vicinity of Janpan, prepared to move on short notice. Two reinforced platoons will be kept ready to polish off any Japs filtering into this area. Extensive patrolling of the trails to the north, south, and west will be maintained.

"Capt. Curl's guerrillas will also aid in the patrolling of this area and will furnish guides to go with Col. Hunter's force.

"Communications will be maintained by radio, runner, and liaison plane with command post which will be at Janpan temporarily."

The 3d Battalion Headquarters with Orange Combat Team was to support Colonel Hunter and to block the trail below Auche leading to Warong and the trails south of Manpin. They were to prevent a flanking Japanese move from the Kamaing area against the Chinese near Shaduzup or against the Marauders near Inkangahtawng.

Inkangahtawng Block

In the afternoon of 21 March Colonel Hunter's force headed south from Janpan, arriving the next day at Auche (Map No. 13, page 64). The 3d Battalion Headquarters and Orange Combat Team followed the main column.

During the night of 22 March General Merrill, at his Janpan headquarters, received from General Stilwell a radio message which said: "Japs withdrawing down the road. Jambu Bum fell today. Come fast now." Because of the success of the Chinese 22d Division at Jambu Bum, General Merrill ordered the 2d Battalion and Khaki Combat Team to arrive at the Kamaing Road 36 hours earlier than he had originally planned.

On 23 March, Colonel Hunter's men pressed rapidly forward to

A "BORROWED" ELEPHANT EQUIPPED WITH A NATIVE RACK
carries the packages which Marauders and Kachins pick up from the drop field at Kaulun Ga.

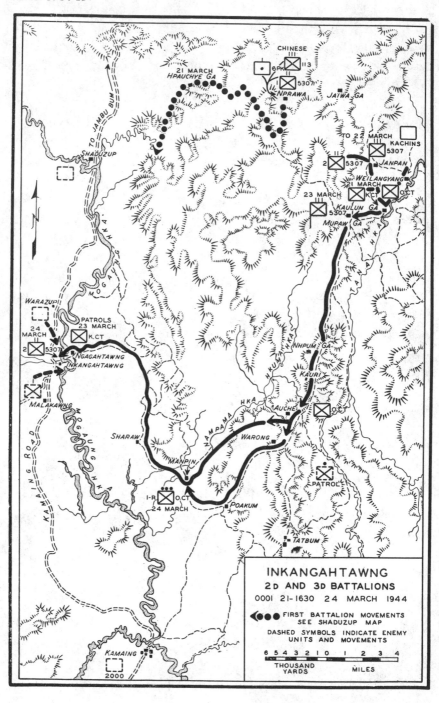

INKANGAHTAWNG
2D AND 3D BATTALIONS
0001 21-1630 24 MARCH 1944

◄●●● FIRST BATTALION MOVEMENTS
SEE SHADUZUP MAP
DASHED SYMBOLS INDICATE ENEMY
UNITS AND MOVEMENTS

6 5 4 3 2 1 0 1 2 3 4
THOUSAND   MILES
YARDS

maintain their new schedule. In order to avoid possible enemy patrols on main routes, they left the trail at Auche to follow the Nampama River as far as Manpin. From there they took up the trail leading through Sharaw into the flat Mogaung Valley.

Patrols from the 2d Battalion clashed with Japanese near Inkangahtawng, and scouts reported a company of enemy dug in near the village, apparently alerted and being reinforced. The 2d Battalion waded the Mogaung River, pushed forward as far as it could, and in the face of increasing opposition dug in about ¼ mile north of Inkangahtawng and 300 yards east of the Kamaing Road, between the road and the river. Khaki Combat Team moved to a position on the east bank of the river where it could protect the rear of the 2d Battalion, assist the battalion with mortar fire, and patrol eastward.

Colonel Hunter planned that the 2d Battalion would throw up a road block at Inkangahtawng, would send patrols north to contact troops from the Chinese 113th Regiment which should be working down from Shaduzup, and would cut the road again south of Inkangahtawng toward Kamaing. Khaki Combat Team would be held in reserve. He had expected this whole operation to tie in with the thrust which the 1st Battalion was making near Shaduzup. According to the original plans, the two simultaneous attacks on the Japanese-held road would support each other by dividing the enemy's attention. Word that the 1st Battalion was delayed and would be unable to carry out its mission on schedule came too late to modify the over-all plan.

Shortly after daylight on 24 March, Colonel McGee sent two reinforced platoons of his 2d Battalion to envelope the village of Inkangahtawng. These platoons struck heavily fortified positions too strong for them to handle, and McGee ordered them to withdraw before they became inextricably involved.

At 0700 the 2d Battalion's left flank was attacked heavily from the road. Kunai grass, 6 to 8 feet high, offered the Japanese excellent cover within which to assemble small groups for a charge. For 15 minutes heavy mortar fire fell on the Marauder position, then, as the mortar fire slackened, the enemy charged from the kunai grass. At a range of 20 yards the whole Marauder perimeter opened fire. Only a few of the Japanese ever reached the defending line: one was killed by a Marauder in his fox hole after a brief wrestling match;

the head of a lieutenant, blown completely off, rolled into another fox hole. Met by this deadly fire, the attack wilted and collapsed.

During the next 3 hours the Japanese repeatedly attacked from the north. Sgt. Norman H. Willey's Pioneer and Demolition Platoon bore the brunt of these attacks and repulsed them all. In the afternoon the Japanese, slipping in close to the river, assaulted the perimeter from the south, using mortar, machine-gun, and artillery preparation.

The men of the 2d Battalion were running low in ammunition and were in danger of being cut off from the rear. Movement of enemy trucks could be heard, bringing up reinforcements thought to be from Kamaing. The Japanese attacking from the north had artillery. A radio message was intercepted from the 1st Battalion to General Merrill, indicating that the 1st Battalion had not yet arrived at Shaduzup; the enemy was therefore free to concentrate against the Marauders at Inkangahtawng. McGee's orders had been to hold the block for 24 hours, but not to stay longer if this would endanger his force. In view of the situation, he decided at 1630 to withdraw toward Manpin. Khaki Combat Team held a bridgehead and kept its mortars hot until the 2d Battalion crossed to the east bank of the Mogaung River (Map No. 14, page 67). Then both units withdrew to Ngagahtawng, where they bivouacked. Four platoons, which McGee had sent in advance of the main force, had blocked all trails to the east and placed booby traps around the circumference of the bivouac. Colonel Hunter, engaged in keeping the line of communications open, was at Sharaw and did not know of the retirement.

Establishing and holding their perimeter for 24 hours to block the Kamaing Road had cost the Marauders 2 killed and 12 wounded. Known enemy dead numbered more than 200.

The Japanese Strike Toward the Tanai Valley

Even apart from the check at Inkangahtawng, the operations planned for Colonel Hunter's forces were disrupted by intelligence which had reached Unit headquarters (Map No. 14, page 67). From a captured Japanese map General Merrill had learned that a strong Japanese force, possibly two battalions, was expected to move from Kamaing to the Tanai Valley, advance north in that area, and then turn westward to attack the flank of the Chinese 22d Division near Shaduzup. General Stilwell ordered General Merrill to block this

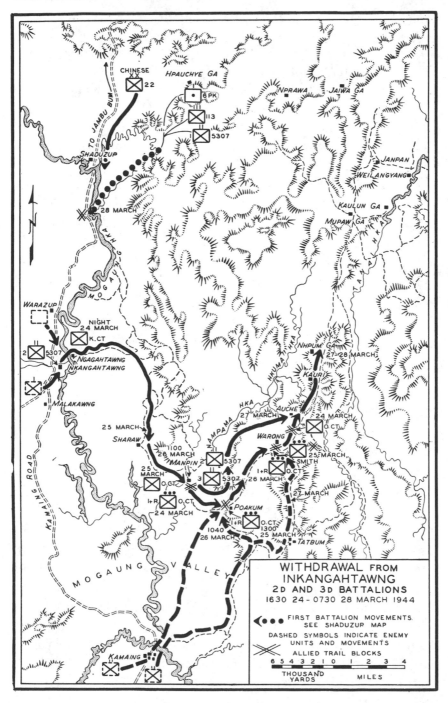

CHINESE 22

HPAUCHYE GA

6 PK

113

5307

TO JAMBU BUM

NPRAWA   JAIWA GA

SHADUZUP

JANPAN

WEILANGYANG

28 MARCH

KAULUN GA

MUPAW GA

WARAZUP

NIGHT
24 MARCH
K.CT

2 5307

NGAGAHTAWNG
NKANGAHTAWNG

MALAKAWNG

NHPUM GA
27-28 MARCH

KAURI

AUCHE

25 MARCH
SHARAW

1100
26 MARCH
MANPIN 2 5307

NAMPAMA HKA

HKUMA HKA

TANAI HKA

24 MARCH
O.CT

25 MARCH

SMITH

WARONG

1+R   O.CT
26 MARCH

25
MARCH
O.CT

3 5307

27 MARCH

1+R   O.CT
24 MARCH

POAKUM

1+R   O.CT
1300

KIMAING ROAD

1040
26 MARCH

25 MARCH
TATBUM

MOGAUNG   VALLEY

WITHDRAWAL FROM
INKANGAHTAWNG
2D AND 3D BATTALIONS
1630 24 - 0730 28 MARCH 1944

⏴•••   FIRST BATTALION MOVEMENTS.
         SEE SHADUZUP MAP
         DASHED SYMBOLS INDICATE ENEMY
         UNITS AND MOVEMENTS
         ALLIED TRAIL BLOCKS

6 5 4 3 2 1 0   1   2   3   4

THOUSAND
YARDS   MILES

KAMAING

67

move and to prevent any Japanese advance beyond Nhpum Ga. During 25 March, this information reached the units scattered on the trails between Ngagahtawng and Warong. Because of difficulties in communications, the first messages came to battalion commanders, and Colonel Hunter was late in getting word of the changed situation.

On the morning of the 25th, the 2d Battalion and Khaki Combat Team resumed their withdrawal eastward from the Inkangahtawng area. Carrying their wounded on litters and hampered by rough country and torrential rains, they reached Sharaw that afternoon; there they were able to evacuate the wounded men by liaison planes. At noon Colonel McGee received a brief message from General Merrill, warning him that a Japanese movement from Kamaing, in more than battalion strength, was threatening his rear and flank.

Meanwhile Colonel Beach, unaware of the new developments, was moving west toward Manpin with Orange Combat Team. His mission had been to protect the rear of the units which were advancing on Inkangahtawng, and he had established a block on the Warong-Auche trail. Hearing on the 24th that the 2d Battalion had reached the Kamaing Road, Colonel Beach started west to join the main force at Inkangahtawng. The bulk of Orange Combat Team reached Manpin at 1030 on the 25th. Here it received word from General Merrill of the Japanese threat toward the Tanai Valley. Colonel Beach immediately took measures to cover the trails leading from Kamaing toward Nhpum Ga and thereby protect the Marauders' route of withdrawal. He sent Lieutenant Weston's I and R Platoon about 2 miles eastward to place a block on the Poakum trail, and a rifle platoon under Lt. Warren R. Smith to watch the Warong-Tatbum trail south of Warong. Weston's men reached Poakum at 1300, sent back for a section of mortars and one of machine guns, and by evening were dug in and ready for action. Smith's platoon reached Poakum at dark, spent the night there, and went on toward Warong early next morning.

When an officer from Orange Combat Team reached him, Colonel Hunter learned for the first time of the warning from higher headquarters. Its meaning was not clear to him; from Kachin patrols toward Kamaing he knew that no movement toward the Tanai had started. On radioing General Merrill for permission to stay at Manpin, Colonel Hunter was directed to proceed to Nhpum Ga.

On 26 March, with the platoons of Weston and Smith covering the southern flank, the 2d and 3d Battalions started their march toward Auche.[16] The 2d Battalion reached Manpin before noon, received a much needed drop of rations and ammunition, and went on nearly 5 miles. The 3d Battalion followed from Manpin next morning. The trail through Poakum and Warong would expose the flank of the withdrawal to the expected enemy attack, so the battalions again used the difficult route up the gorge of the Nampama River, which involved some 40 river crossings and was exhausting for the troops.

Before the 2d Battalion left Manpin, word was received that the enemy move was under way toward the Tanai Valley. Colonel Hunter learned at 1615 from scouts that the Japanese were starting north from Kamaing in motor trucks, which could use the wide trails for some distance. He called for an air attack by a fighter mission on patrol in the area, and their action helped to delay the enemy's move. However, forward elements of the Japanese force had already reached Poakum and were hotly engaged there with Lieutenant Weston's I and R Platoon.

Lieutenant Weston's fight began at 1040, when a weak advance party of Japanese approached Poakum on the Kamaing trail and was easily turned back. At 1130 an attack in company strength, made both on the trail and to the west of the village, was finally broken up by mortar fire. At 1400 a still heavier assault was made from three sides. Though it was held off, Lieutenant Weston estimated that the enemy force was now so large that he might be outflanked and encircled. After putting a heavy concentration of mortar fire on enemy assembly areas, the platoon pulled out of Poakum at 1520 and withdrew successfully toward Warong. Arriving there at 1800, the I and R Platoon joined Lieutenant Smith's rifle platoon and organized for a further delaying action. The combined forces numbered about 90 men. They had no radio communications, the only radio having been knocked out by enemy mortar fire at Poakum.

No enemy approached Warong until next morning, 27 March. Between 1000 and 1100 the Marauders' defenses were tested not only on the trail from Poakum but on the Tatbum trail. Strong enemy forces were converging on Warong by both routes. It took several hours for the Japanese to feel out the Marauder positions, and the first attacks were repulsed. By 1500 it appeared that the enemy was

---

[16] Colonel Hunter's force was now dissolved; Khaki Combat Team rejoined the 3d Battalion.

not only ready for an assault in strength but had shifted a force estimated at company strength west around Warong near the trail leading toward Auche. This threatened the escape route of the Marauder platoons, and a withdrawal was decided on. A messenger mounted on their only mule was sent back to notify General Merrill. The force was organized in two teams and about 1630 began to displace northward by successive bounds, one team holding while the other organized a stand further in the rear. These tactics held off the enemy and allowed the tired platoons to reach Auche by dark. Despite 2 days of fighting against an enemy much greater in numbers, the Marauder platoons had suffered no casualties.

Their action had been effective in covering the withdrawal of the main Marauder forces. On the 27th the 2d Battalion had reached Auche at 0930 and stayed there while the 3d Battalion went through and on toward the north. The troops at Auche set up defensive perimeters for the night and took precautions against possible infiltration from the direction of Warong.

28 March saw the last and hardest stage of the Marauders' withdrawal toward the Tanai Valley. At 0600 Khaki Combat Team started for Nhpum Ga, with Blue Combat Team a short distance behind. At 0630 the 2d Battalion headquarters and Green Combat Team were just pulling out of Auche when two enemy shells landed at the edge of the village. A moment later two more shells landed uncomfortably close to them.

The prospect facing the Marauders was extremely unsatisfactory. Between Auche and Nhpum Ga the trail was along the crest of a narrow ridge. Its precipitous sides, covered with rank growth, gave no room for dispersal, and it soon became evident that the enemy, from the vicinity of Warong, was using observed fire.

As the tail of the Marauders' column cleared Auche, a third pair of shells came whistling over. The Japanese had found the range; one man and several animals were hit. A steady stream of artillery fire then poured into the area and searched the trail. Nhpum Ga lay 4½ miles ahead, and most of the trail was uphill. Mud was ankle-deep. Frequently the animals fell. They had to be unloaded before they could regain their feet, and then repacked. Word to "move faster" ran up and down the column, which already was moving at an awkward run. Medics were ordered to the rear where

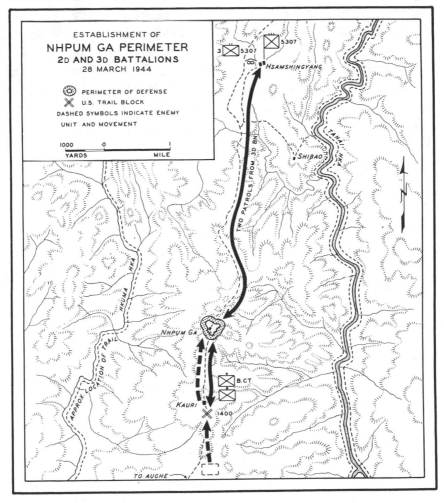

ESTABLISHMENT OF
NHPUM GA PERIMETER
2D AND 3D BATTALIONS
28 MARCH 1944

⊙ PERIMETER OF DEFENSE
☒ U.S. TRAIL BLOCK
DASHED SYMBOLS INDICATE ENEMY
UNIT AND MOVEMENT

they were kept busy. An hour and a half after leaving Auche, the 2d Battalion reached Nhpum Ga.

The exertion of the last few days had told heavily on the unit. The round trip from Nhpum Ga to Inkangahtawng was approximately 70 miles, and had included a hard fight at the Kamaing Road followed by forced marches. The last uphill dash from Auche through mud and bursting shells was particularly exhausting.

Nhpum Ga

General Merrill ordered the 2d Battalion to establish and hold a defensive perimeter at Nhpum Ga to stop the Japanese from advancing beyond that point (Map No. 15, above). He directed that the 3d Battalion move to Hsamshingyang, about 5 miles to the north. There this battalion was to protect a field for supply drops and an air strip for evacuation planes, as well as to block the trails against any surprise attack from the north. Combat patrols would be sent east of the Tanai River to keep the Japanese from bypassing Nhpum Ga and continuing toward Shaduzup. The 3d Battalion was also to send two patrols daily to Nhpum Ga. The patrols were to keep the trail open and to carry any wounded men of the 2d Battalion back to Hsamshingyang.

Four or five native huts, occupied mainly during the monsoon period, make up the village of Nhpum Ga. It lies on the highest ground, 2,800 feet above sea level, of a knobby ridge between the Tanai and Hkuma watersheds. The north-south trail, following the narrow crest of the ridge, meets at Nhpum Ga a path running down to the Hkuma River, 1½ miles to the west. East of the village the ridge has abrupt slopes cut by ravines which lead to the Tanai River, 2 miles away and 1,400 feet below the village. In both side valleys were trails which might be used by the Japanese to bypass Nhpum Ga.

The 2d Battalion took hurried measures to organize their defense against expected pursuit from the south (Sketch No. 2, page 73). The Nhpum Ga huts lay on a small knoll just off the intersection of the trail leading west, with commanding ground close by on either side. East was a knob, 50 feet higher than the trail; westward, dominating both trails, was a narrow hill running north to south. Both features would be important in defending Nhpum Ga, but the 2d Battalion's first concern was with the approaches from the south. Here, the trail came up toward the village along a gently sloping nose of ground, with a steep-sided draw to the west, covered with heavy jungle. Blue Combat Team set up positions to include this nose and defend its eastern flank. A machine gun was placed 100 yards down the western trail, and outposts were put on the key high ground near the village, to watch the flanks and rear. For the start, the south was the threatened area.

Colonel McGee was not given long to set up defenses. Two platoons, one at Kauri and one further north, had been left to put up delaying fights along the trail. They were forced back earlier than had been expected, and by 1400 were in the perimeter with the Japanese following close behind.

At 1605 Japanese artillery and mortar fire began searching out the southern tip of the 2d Battalion's perimeter. A few minutes later came an infantry assault. This attack, easily repulsed, was obviously a feeling-out operation, and the Marauders held their automatic fire in order not to disclose their strength. It was believed that a heavy shock attack was imminent, and the men of the 2d Battalion utilized every moment to strengthen and improve their positions.

During the night of 28/29 March, occasional mortar and artillery fire fell into the perimeter. Doubtless intended to harass the defenders and keep them awake, the fire failed to accomplish this result. The

SKETCH NO. 2

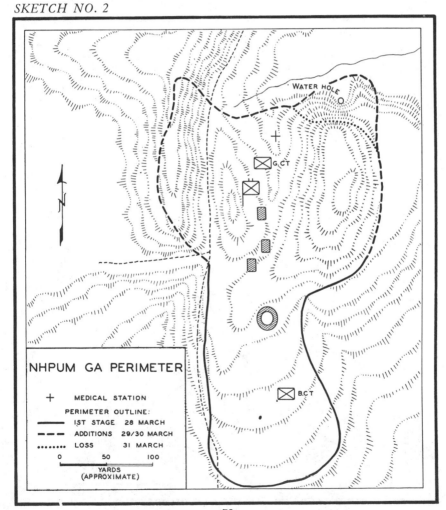

NHPUM GA PERIMETER

+   MEDICAL STATION

PERIMETER OUTLINE:

———   IST STAGE   28 MARCH
– – –   ADDITIONS   29/30 MARCH
·······   LOSS   31 MARCH

0   50   100
YARDS
(APPROXIMATE)

majority of the 2d Battalion men were so exhausted that nothing short of a direct hit could have aroused those not actually required to guard the two-man fox holes in the perimeter. In these one man slept while the other remained alert. An infiltrating night attack was greatly feared and would have been especially dangerous in view of the Marauders' condition, but the enemy failed to seize this opportunity.

On 29 March Colonel Hunter assumed command of the 5307th; General Merrill had become seriously ill and was awaiting evacuation from Hsamshingyang.

At daylight the Japanese again opened up with artillery and mortars (Map No. 16, below and Sketch No. 2, page 73). A

MAP NO. 16

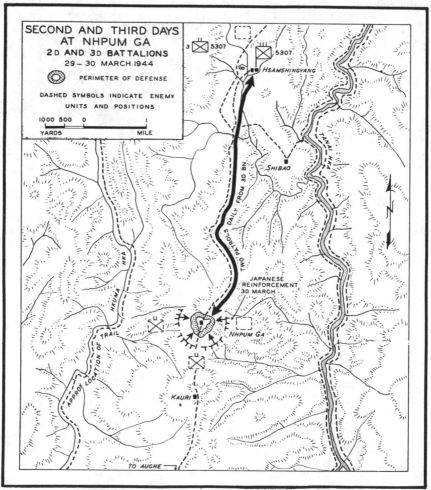

SECOND AND THIRD DAYS
AT NHPUM GA
2D AND 3D BATTALIONS
29 – 30 MARCH 1944

PERIMETER OF DEFENSE

DASHED SYMBOLS INDICATE ENEMY
UNITS AND POSITIONS

1000 500 0
YARDS   MILE

machine-gun barrage preceded an attack at 0600 from the southeast. This thrust accomplished nothing for the enemy; neither did one from the southwest at 1000, nor a third at 1500 from almost due south. All three attacks followed the same pattern.

At 1515 and again at 1750 McGee, concerned about the trail to the north of the perimeter, radioed to unit headquarters at Hsamshingyang to see if the 3d Battalion could help at Nhpum Ga. No help was then available at Hsamshingyang. The 3d Battalion was needed at Hsamshingyang to defend the air strip and to stop any Japanese movement along the Tanai north of Nhpum Ga. Colonel Hunter told McGee that the 3d Battalion would continue to keep the trail open by sending a platoon combat patrol twice daily from the air strip to Nhpum Ga.

By nightfall it was evident that the Japanese were digging in for a siege. At 1750 light artillery fire commenced. Then the enemy's mortars and machine guns opened up, and his infantry struck at the perimeter's southwest corner. Again the attack failed.

The 2d Battalion expected more determined assaults and was beginning to worry about its flanks. Throughout the day the men in the perimeter had heard sounds indicating that the Japanese were moving west of Nhpum Ga near the side trail. During the evening Colonel McGee learned from Colonel Hunter that the enemy was moving down the Tanai Valley in large numbers and that probably at least a battalion was making the attack along the Nhpum Ga trail.[17] Measures were taken to meet the flanking threats, and the perimeter was enlarged to include the high ground on both sides of the village. In improving and extending the positions, the digging was done at night and cautiously, for the Japanese had a trick of worming their way close to the perimeter to hurl grenades at any spot where they heard voices or sounds of activity.

Back at Hsamshingyang the 3d Battalion spent the night patrolling all avenues of approach to the air strip. One group of Japanese that tried to circle northward to the rear of the field was hit hard and turned back. Kachin guerrillas, busy scouting around the strip, frequently ambushed small enemy parties. The Kachins were probably of more assistance than anyone realized, by creating in the minds

---

[17] This force was later identified by papers taken from Japanese bodies as a reinforced battalion of the 114th Regiment and elements of the 55th Regiment.

of the Japanese an exaggerated idea of the size of the area held by the Marauders and of their strength.

At Nhpum Ga Japanese artillery, machine-gun, and mortar fire opened with the dawn of 30 March. This time the eastern side of the perimeter was attacked in greater force than in any previous engagement, and the attack persisted despite the Marauders' heavy defensive fires. When this effort finally slackened, the Japanese closed in again a little later from farther north. Again they failed, and once more, after an attack had been repelled, the spirits of the defenders rose. During the day the Japanese located the position of the Marauders' mortars, and the enemy artillery began systematically to blast the rise which masked the mortars.

Developed progressively to meet the extending enemy attacks, the perimeter had now assumed an elongated shape, about 400 yards long and broadening in the northern half to include the key high ground on both sides of the trail. Green Combat Team held the western and northern side. The battalion's aid station had been placed just north of the village, on a slope partly protected from enemy shells by the small knoll. Fox holes were prepared large enough to accommodate litters and permit medical attention for the wounded. The trail to Hsamshingyang was still open; Sgt. John Keslik's patrol arrived from the 3d Battalion and stayed within the perimeter for the night. All litter cases had been carried to the airfield for evacuation. Within the perimeter living conditions were becoming extremely unpleasant. Since the first day enemy artillery had played havoc with the Marauders' animals, which could not be dug in. They had been put into the area between the knoll and the hill just west of the trail, and north of the knoll, but the ground gave no protection against the effects of tree bursts. Of 200 horses and mules, about 75 had been killed, and their carcasses after lying for 2 days on the ground had begun to putrefy. From beyond the perimeter the wind brought the smell of Japanese corpses which were already decomposing. The stench was almost insufferable.

Beginning of the Siege

31 March saw a full test of the Nhpum Ga defenses. The enemy barrage which started the day was not exceptionally heavy, but the attack that followed came from three points at once: south, east, and northwest of the perimeter (Map No. 17, page 77). On the west,

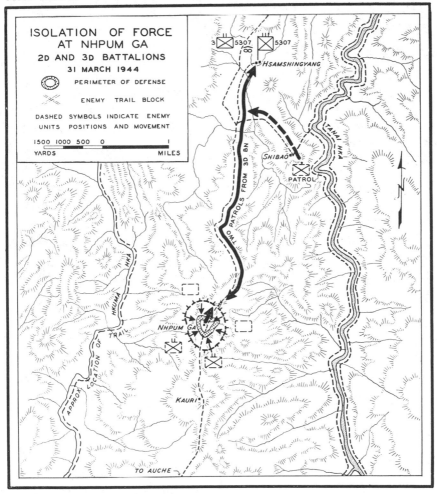

ISOLATION OF FORCE
AT NHPUM GA
2D AND 3D BATTALIONS
31 MARCH 1944
PERIMETER OF DEFENSE
ENEMY TRAIL BLOCK
DASHED SYMBOLS INDICATE ENEMY
UNITS POSITIONS AND MOVEMENT
1500 1000 500 0
YARDS
MILES

ₐn enemy attack overran the machine-gun outpost on the side trail;
Green Combat Team strengthened its perimeter along the hill protecting the village on that flank. The strongest enemy effort came
from the north. Here a wide draw, followed by a sluggish brook,
led up toward the rear of the Marauders' position. Even using
everybody available, including mule skinners and headquarters personnel, the battalion had not had enough men to extend the perimeter to the far side of the draw. Using this approach, the enemy
thrust at the knob which formed the northeast buttress of the perimeter. The knob sloped very steeply down to the draw; in a little
hollow, just under these slopes, lay the water hole supplying the

entire Marauder force. In an hour of hot fighting, the Japanese forced the Pioneer and Demolition Platoon back up the knob. A counterattack failed to dislodge the enemy from the ground controlling the hollow, and the water hole was lost.

As the direction of the Japanese attack indicated, communications with Hsamshingyang were also lost. At 0800 the usual morning patrol had been dispatched from Hsamshingyang by Orange Combat Team. This time the patrol, led by Lieutenant Smith, detected numerous signs that the enemy had used the trail through most of its length. When the party reached a point 400 yards from McGee's perimeter, it was fired upon from a strong enemy trail block which had been established during the night. The Marauders halted to organize for a break-through attempt and during the halt established communications by radio with the leader of Blue Combat Team's weapons platoon within the perimeter. Lieutenant Smith directed Blue Combat Team's mortar fire upon the trail block and attacked with his patrol. The attack failed.

Unable to contact Colonel Hunter by radio, Lieutenant Smith sent two messengers to Hsamshingyang requesting reinforcements for assaulting the block. These messengers were ambushed before they had gone 300 yards. The patrol had to return to Hsamshingyang through the jungle and along the bed of a stream running due west. The Japanese pursued on both sides of the stream-bed and had to be fought off in delaying actions.

About 1000, Colonel McGee learned that the enemy had cut the trail to Hsamshingyang and that his position was completely encircled. He was told that patrols from the 3d Battalion hoped to dislodge the block by noon; but he soon heard that this effort had failed to get through. Colonel McGee then decided to attempt breaking the Japanese block from his end of the trail. Carefully he thinned out his entire line and organized a task force approximating a reinforced platoon in strength. Supported by mortar and machine-gun fire, this force struck hard, but within 200 yards of the perimeter it ran into prepared enemy positions. After suffering several casualties it had to withdraw. At 1600 McGee radioed Colonel Hunter that his rear was blocked and that he would like "something" to relieve the enemy pressure isolating his force at Nhpum Ga.

An air drop furnished the 2d Battalion with plenty of food and ammunition, but the water shortage quickly became serious. Cut off from the water hole, the Marauders could still get into the draw just north of the perimeter, where small swampy pools had been used for the animals. Dead mules lay in the draw, adding the taste of decomposed flesh to the water. Nevertheless, the Marauders dug a shallow pit to conserve the nauseous liquid.

During this same day, 31 March, a strong Japanese patrol pressed from the southeast toward the air strip at Hsamshingyang, vital for supply and evacuation of the two battalions. When this group ran into one of the patrols from Orange Combat Team, the sound of shots quickly brought reinforcements from the team and the enemy

MAP NO. 18

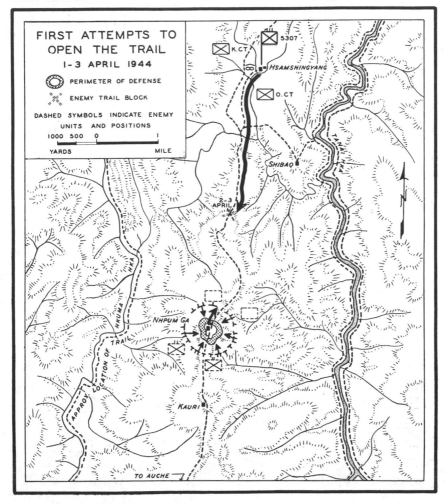

79

group was pushed back after a sharp fight in which several Marauders were killed and 12 wounded.

The Japanese omitted their customary artillery salute to dawn on 1 April (Map No. 18, below). The respite for the Marauders was short: when they laid a mortar concentration on the enemy near the water hole, enemy artillery answered at 0900, and this time from positions near Kauri, within a range of 1,000 yards. After a relatively light barrage enemy units attacked simultaneously from the east and northeast. Both attacks failed to gain any more ground.

The Japanese could not penetrate the perimeter from the northeast, but they still held the water hole very strongly. The 2d Battalion had no immediate hope of getting it back, and the shortage of water within the perimeter was so grave that the doctors had none for making plaster casts and were forced to give patients sulphadiazine dry. In desperation Colonel McGee requested an air drop of 500 gallons in plastic bags.

This day was marked for the beleaguered 2d Battalion by the receipt of a cheering message. The success of the Marauders at Shaduzup was now known, and the 2d Battalion was congratulated for contributing to this by its road block at Inkangahtawng. But the conclusion drawn from the Shaduzup action, in a message from Colonel Hunter, was: "Nips running like hell from Shaduzup. Too many dead to be counted. Expect your friends to pull out tonight or tomorrow morning. Mortar the hell out of them. Lew will pursue if feasible." Events of the next few days would make this forecast look like an "April Fool."

Whatever the enemy intentions might be, Colonel Hunter and the 3d Battalion were making an attempt to relieve Nhpum Ga. Though his entire force was none too adequate for defense of the Hsamshingyang area and the vital air strip, Colonel Hunter had decided to use Orange Combat Team to reopen the trail to the 2d Battalion. The attempt began on 1 April and at first showed good progress. Though the Japanese had now sifted up the trail close to Hsamshingyang, they were not present in strength. Orange Combat Team fought past two blocks and made nearly 2 miles.

On 2 April the going became harder. Following along the ridge crest, the trail from Hsamshingyang rises nearly 1,000 feet before reaching Nhpum Ga. The height is gained unevenly, in a series of sharp rises between which the ridge line runs level. Orange Combat Team, after making a good start against light resistance, came to one of the steep sections on the trail and found the Japanese dug in, ready to hold. In the initial encounter, two lead scouts were killed and Cpl. Frank L. Graham was wounded after he had killed some of the crew of an enemy machine gun. Platoon attacks by Orange knocked out several machine guns but found others in higher positions, well sited to cover all approaches near the trail. The ridge crest at this point was only 75 yards wide, and the steep slopes on either side of the ridge were covered with heavy jungle, making it difficult to use flanking maneuvers. For the moment the Marauders were stopped, halfway to their goal. Reopening the trail would require a major effort.

In one respect the day saw a considerable improvement in the Marauders' situation. Subjected for several days to the harassing fire of the enemy guns, the 2d and 3d Battalions had keenly felt the need for artillery of their own. When General Merrill was evacuated to Ledo, he had ordered two 75-mm howitzers dispatched at once to the 3d Battalion at Hsamshingyang. The Marauders' rear echelon outdid itself in carrying out his instructions with all possible speed. At 0930 on 2 April the two field pieces, in bulky chunks dangling from double parachutes, dropped to the Hsamshingyang air strip.

ONE OF THE MARAUDERS' TWO 75-MM HOWITZERS *goes into action.*

The men of the hard-pressed 2d Battalion at Nhpum Ga could plainly see this air drop 4 miles away and were cheered by the sight.

Colonel Hunter, meanwhile, had assembled two gun crews, composed of men who had been with the 98th Pack Artillery in New Guinea. S/Sgt. John A. Acker acted as battery commander. He had formed the two crews and had put them through intensive refresher practice so that they were well-drilled when the howitzers came floating down to them. Two hours after the planes had dropped the artillery pieces, the first round sailed out over the 2d Battalion's perimeter. Soon both guns were registering on enemy positions.

The main effort on 3 April was made by the beleaguered 2d Battalion. Colonel Hunter instructed it to make a strong attack north from the Nhpum Ga hill in an attempt to contact Orange Combat Team. An artillery barrage and air support would aid the attack. McGee's men did their best, but the net result was no gain. After 7 days of battle and siege, the situation at Nhpum Ga was unchanged. Some of the wounded, who could not be evacuated, had died: six men were buried next morning within the perimeter. A large proportion of the men now had dysentery and stomach disorders. The 500 gallons of water, requested on 1 April, had come by air drop, and this relieved the most desperate aspect of the battalion's position. Rations and ammunition were dropped regularly by transports. Some of these supplies drifted over to the Japanese lines, but no large amount was lost.

The 3d Battalion Increases its Effort

At 1500 on 3 April Colonel Hunter called a staff meeting to go over the situation. The 2d Battalion had now been surrounded for 4 days. By infiltrating the enemy lines in small groups, most of the able-bodied men could probably have got through to Hsamshing-yang; this had been demonstrated when Sergeant Keslik's patrol, after staying 2 days in the perimeter (page 76), had succeeded in rejoining Orange Combat Team. However, this procedure would have involved sacrificing the wounded men and losing all animals and heavy weapons. McGee's force was receiving supplies regularly and was judged to be in fair shape except for means of evacuating the wounded and protecting its animals.

Colonel Hunter had to consider not only the situation of the 2d Battalion but the execution of his mission, which was to prevent the

Japanese advance from striking west from the Tanai Valley toward Shaduzup. A considerable part of the enemy force was being held up at Nhpum Ga, but there were still reports of enemy movement east of the Tanai River. If strong Japanese forces used the Tanai Valley to get past Nhpum Ga, Colonel Hunter had to be ready to block them off at the points where they might swing west on trails toward Shaduzup. There were two such points: one near Hsamshingyang, and another further north at Weilangyang. Colonel Hunter faced the possibility of having to move the 3d Battalion to meet any serious enemy threat in either area.

Reinforcement for the two battalions was obviously needed but could not be expected for some time. An urgent message had been sent asking for support from the 1st Battalion, but the message had been delayed by communication troubles and did not reach the battalion until that very day, 3 April (page 59). The 1st Battalion could not reach Hsamshingyang before 7 April. Capt. John B. George of 3d Battalion Headquarters, accompanied by T/Sgt. Lawrence J. Hill and Sgt. Lum K. Pun, a Chinese interpreter, had been sent to Weilangyang to ask assistance from a battalion of the Chinese 112th Regiment. However, this unit also could not be expected to arrive for several days.

After discussing all aspects of the situation, Col. Hunter made his decision in these words:

"Gentlemen, in the morning we start an attack that will drive through to the 2d Battalion. It may take two or three days, but we *will* get through. All troops except the sick and the mule skinners will be withdrawn from the air strip. [All] large patrols will be called in, and Kachins substituted wherever possible. Tomorrow, as soon as we can get ready, Orange Combat Team will attack due south along the trail. [The men of] Khaki Combat Team will leave their heavy equipment here, march due south behind Orange Combat Team until they are 400 yards from Jap position, then turn west down the mountain and attack the Japs on their west flank. The artillery will be moved up to where it can fire point blank into the Jap bunkers and pill boxes. Every man of the gun crews volunteered . . . this afternoon. This attack will be tentatively set for 1200 tomorrow. Ruses, feints, and anything else you can do to fool the Japs are in order. A fake message will be dropped from a plane so as to fall in the Jap lines. This message will be to the 2d Battalion and will say that a battalion of parachutists will be dropped between

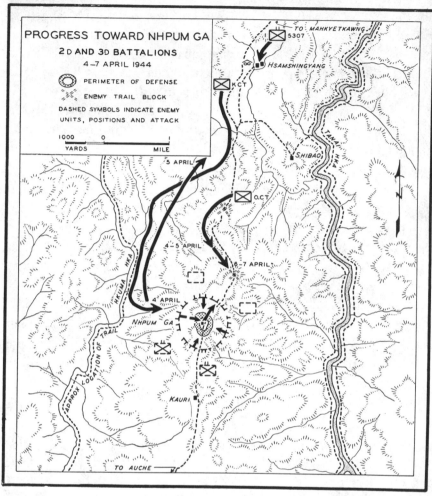

Kauri and Auche at 1700 hours tomorrow (4 April). If possible we will have a dummy drop [of supplies] in that area to fool them."

The morning of 4 April was taken up with preparations for the new attack (Map No. 19, page 84). Because the air strip was to be left virtually undefended when the 3d Battalion started its drive toward Nhpum Ga, Colonel Hunter moved his command headquarters 2 miles further north to Mahkyetkawng. There the headquarters group met a platoon of Chinese, the advance element of the battalion which Captain George had contacted at Weilangyang. These Chinese were directed to dig in and to hold the trail junction at Mahkyetkawng.

Colonel Hunter himself joined Orange Combat Team for the new push against the trail block. Overhead, planes were dive-bombing and strafing wherever they could find a target. They were also directed by ground radios to targets that could not be seen from the air. At 1100 it became evident that, because of the difficulties Khaki Combat Team was having in cutting through the jungle, the attack could not jump off at noon as scheduled. Colonel Hunter postponed it to 1600. He was extremely anxious not to attack until he had organized all the strength under his command.

At 1530 the Pioneer and Demolition Platoon, carrying out Colonel Hunter's plans, began a fake fight west of the point where Orange Combat Team would make the main attack. The Japanese obligingly shifted their mortars to throw fire in that direction. American planes appeared at 1545, and at 1605 the Marauders' artillery and mortars opened up. Enemy resistance was overcome by these preparatory fires; when Orange Combat Team advanced on the narrow front across the ridge top, its attack carried up the steep knob and several hundred yards on the level stretch beyond. No casualties were suffered until the advance was stopped toward dark by fire from a new enemy block. Here Major Lew, commanding Orange Combat Team, was severely wounded.

The gain was encouraging, but it soon became evident the enemy

AN ORANGE COMBAT TEAM MORTAR CREW, *dug in between Nhpum Ga and Hsamshingyang, fires on the Japanese trail-block positions.*

was still prepared to fight on successive delaying positions. He held the Marauders to no gain on 5 April. Despite several attacks, Orange was unable to advance against fire from commanding positions on a small side hill, which flanked the trail to the left of the main ridge.

In the attack of 4 April, Khaki Combat Team had met with no success on its wide flanking maneuver. Major Briggs had equipped two platoons with all the light machine guns and mortars that could be spared. He led them along the trail toward Nhpum Ga, then veered west, cutting a path along the jungle-covered mountain slopes to a point west of the 2d Battalion's defenses. The men were badly slowed by being forced to cross a succession of rough spurs running west toward the Hkuma Valley. When the platoons tried to drive up toward the perimeter they were stopped by bands of fire from well dug-in enemy positions. Patrols were sent to feel out the enemy flanks, but strong resistance and the difficult terrain combined to foil the effort. The two platoons bivouacked where they were for the night. The next day they found themselves threatened in the rear, and to escape had to cut a new trail back to the air strip at Hsamshingyang.

Two days of strenuous effort by the 3d Battalion had not yet lifted the siege, but the effects were beginning to be felt at Nhpum Ga. On 4 April, while the relief attack was in progress, the Japanese made a heavy assault on the hill top from the west and penetrated the 2d Battalion's perimeter for a short distance. At one point a few of the enemy actually reached fox holes behind the defense line. Two Marauders quickly wiped out the Japanese inside the perimeter with hand grenades. The defenders were heartened by their success and took a new grip on themselves.

The following night at 0200 and again at 0430 enemy assaults were made on the western boundary of the perimeter. Both of these were anticipated by Colonel McGee. Probably in order to excite "attack spirit," the Japanese indulged in a great deal of preliminary yelling. Tec. 4 Matsumoto, the man who had tapped the enemy telephone wires at Walawbum, was on the northwest hill and could overhear the orders for the attack in time to inform battalion headquarters. The Marauders were ready for the enemy charges and stopped them with heavy losses.

The enemy made no further attacks on 5 April, although Japanese shells fell intermittently within the perimeter. It appeared that the 3d Battalion's push had considerably relieved the pressure against Nhpum Ga. However, Colonel McGee was unable to spare any men from the 2d Battalion's defenses to assist the efforts of Orange and Khaki Combat Teams. Although the men encircled at Nhpum Ga had a welcome respite from the assaults on their position, they had no assurance that this respite would be long. The trail to Hsamshingyang had now been blocked for 6 days. In that time the 2d Battalion had accumulated casualties of 17 men dead, 97 wounded, and 4 missing. Enemy artillery fire had been particularly troublesome since 1 April, when their guns were moved near Kauri. The Japanese weapons, probably the T–41 75–mm mountain gun, had a flat trajectory and high muzzle velocity; at 1,000-yard range, the shells arrived almost simultaneously with the sound of the gun's fire, and the Marauders had no warning in time to seek cover.

The Relief Force Wins Through

On 6 April Orange Combat Team was only a mile from Nhpum Ga, but this last mile was to be the hardest (Map No. 19, page 84). The trail still led along the narrow ridge top, affording a front wide enough for only one or two platoons to operate. Enemy resistance showed no signs of cracking.

The attack opened well on 6 April, mainly as a result of heavy preparatory fires. Several thousand rounds of overhead fire from heavy machine guns and a rolling barrage from 60-mm and 81-mm mortars were used, as well as 200 rounds of artillery and several strafing and dive-bombing attacks. Lieutenant Woomer, leader of the weapons platoon, gave notable assistance in directing the mortar fire. He had worked his way to within 25 yards of two enemy machine guns which were holding up the attack. From this position he directed the mortars by an SCR 300 until the shells were landing just beyond the target. His next order was: "Deflection correct. Bring it in 25 yards, and if you don't hear from me, you'll know you came this way too far. Then shift it back just a little and you'll be right on it." The next rounds knocked out the enemy guns.

During the preparatory fires, the Japanese had left their positions and sought refuge in the jungle at the side of the ridge. When the fires lifted, there was a spectacular race between the Marauders and the Japanese for the vacated fox holes, and the Marauders won. The success netted 500 yards; then came another check. Once again, the ridge line steepened sharply and the trail led up over a knob which gave the enemy excellent firing positions to the front and the west flank. East of the trail there was a cliff.

Facing the last main rise in their path, the Marauders switched combat teams for the next effort. The I and R Platoon of Orange had been spearheading the advance since 3 April and was left in line for one more day; except for that unit, Khaki Combat Team replaced Orange for the trail fight on 7 April. The efforts of that day, Good Friday, were unsuccessful. Close-in fighting on the knob cost three killed and eight wounded, and the few yards gained had to be given up when positions were consolidated for the night. At Nhpum Ga,

MAP NO. 20

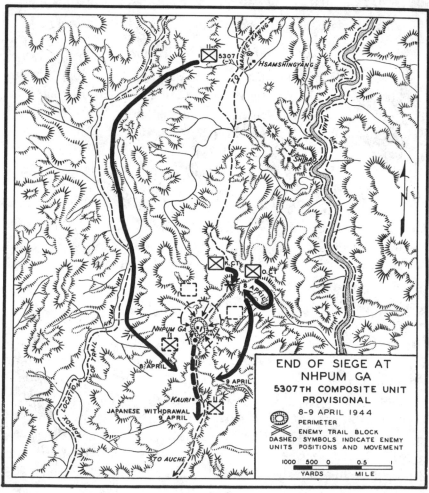

END OF SIEGE AT
NHPUM GA
5307 TH COMPOSITE UNIT
PROVISIONAL
8-9 APRIL 1944
PERIMETER
ENEMY TRAIL BLOCK
DASHED SYMBOLS INDICATE ENEMY
UNITS POSITIONS AND MOVEMENT

McGee's men sustained two enemy attacks in the early morning hours, but the assaults lacked the ferocity and vigor of the earlier enemy efforts. Colonel McGee decided to risk a counterattack north toward the relieving force and scraped together two combat patrols for the attempt. The men were quickly pinned down by fire from the enemy emplacements.

The main event of the 7th was the arrival of the 1st Battalion. Colonel Osborne had received orders on 3 April to press his march to Hsamshingyang, and the 1st Battalion had done its best (Map No. 11, page 48). They made 7 miles on 4 April and did as well on the 5th, when they reached Sintawngkawng. On 6 April, while waiting for an air drop in the late afternoon the battalion picked up another message: the 2d Battalion was engaged in heavy fighting at Nhpum Ga; the 3d Battalion was attempting to reach the 2d Battalion in order to extricate it; and both were in desperate need of support. Spurred by the urgency, the 1st Battalion pushed on again at 1845, covering 5½ miles over the highest hills yet encountered.

At 1700 on 7 April, the 1st Battalion reached Hsamshingyang after a forced march of nearly 4 days. The men were weary and 30 percent were temporarily knocked out by dysentery. Nevertheless, their arrival greatly heartened the exhausted Marauders trying to break the Japanese grip on Nhpum Ga. Capt. Tom P. Senff, now commanding Red Combat Team, was ordered to select those men of the 1st Battalion capable of continued exertion and prepare them for joining the attack on 8 April. He was able to get together 250 men.

Colonel Hunter planned to use his whole force on 8 April (Map No. 20, page 88). Khaki Combat Team would attack the enemy along the trail; Orange Combat Team was to make a flanking effort east of Nhpum Ga along the mountain slopes; Captain Senff's force from the 1st Battalion had the mission of circling Nhpum Ga on the west and creating a diversion at the enemy's rear, south of the perimeter.

Khaki Combat Team had a heartbreaking day of fighting at the knob, with the main burden falling on its I and R Platoon and the 2d Platoon of Company I. The terrain forced the units to make frontal attacks up very steep slopes through thick-growing bamboo, against enemy machine-gun fire and grenades. Five times the platoons tried it, after laying down heavy mortar fire. Four hundred

JAPANESE LIGHT MACHINE GUN, *captured at Nhpum Ga, is examined by the Marauders after the siege. (Left to right the men are: Cpl. Wilbur Thorpe, M/Sgt. Joseph Doyer, 1st Sgt. Henry J. Recke, and S/Sgt. S. F. Rapisarda.)*

rounds of motor shells and something under one hundred of artillery were used during the day. None of the attacks carried more than a few yards. The Marauders suffered about 25 casualties, the I and R Platoon losing 9 men, wounded, out of 22. East of the trail, Orange Combat Team had heavy going in the jungle and was unable to reach the enemy positions.

Captain Senff's force made its wide flanking move as scheduled, passing west of Nhpum Ga and meeting only occasional fire from enemy patrols. At 1800 they were ½ mile south of the perimeter and they bivouacked near the trail connecting Kauri and Nhpum Ga. On their way, the force put blocks along the paths used to supply the Japanese troops west of the perimeter. Two enemy patrols or supply parties stumbled on the bivouac during the night, and early next morning Senff's men located and mortared heavily an enemy bivouac area near Kauri.

Easter Sunday will be memorable in the life of every surviving member of the 2d Battalion. Just after dawn, combat patrols from Khaki Combat Team advanced down the trail without meeting opposition and walked into McGee's perimeter. The enemy had pulled out, apparently discouraged by the tough resistance at Nhpum Ga, the equally determined efforts of the relieving force, and the arrival of reinforcements. The appearance of Senff's force on his flank and rear, disorganizing his communications, may have been a decisive factor. Abandoned equipment and rice still cooking on small fires attested the suddenness of the Japanese departure. No pursuit was undertaken; Captain Senff's force was in position to threaten the Kauri trail, and the I and R Platoon of Orange Combat Team reached it from the east, but General Stilwell had ordered that no advance be made south of Nhpum Ga. The exhausted Marauders limited their efforts to patrolling and cleaning up the scene of the siege. Dead animals and Japanese corpses were buried as quickly as possible; hundreds of pounds of chloride of lime were needed in disinfecting the area. Flamethrowers, used on the bodies of animals, did much to rid the area of the swarms of flies.

The 2d Battalion moved about 20 miles north of Nhpum Ga and set up Battalion Headquarters at Samlulgahtawng. They were ready to lend a hand to the Chinese left guarding the trail near Hsamshingyang in the event that the Japanese grew troublesome. Another battalion of the Chinese 112th Regiment arrived at Hsamshingyang on 22 April.

The total number of Marauder casualties in the Nhpum Ga action was 57 killed and 302 wounded. All those earlier reported missing were found, either killed or wounded. The number evacuated to hospitals by air because of wounds or illness caused by amoebic dysentery and malaria reached a total of 379. The figure of known enemy dead exceeded 400, excluding any estimate of the number of Japanese buried during the 10 days the enemy controlled the area surrounding the 2d Battalion's perimeter.

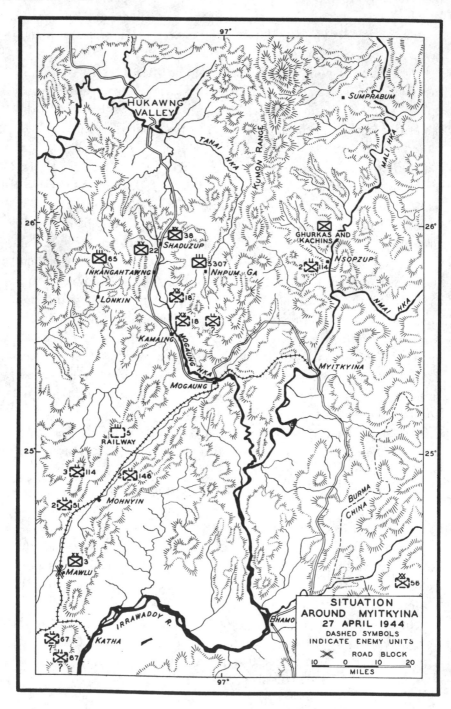

SITUATION
AROUND MYITKYINA
27 APRIL 1944
DASHED SYMBOLS
INDICATE ENEMY UNITS

ROAD BLOCK

10   0   10   20
MILES

Third Mission: Myitkyina

BY LATE APRIL, the Allied offensive in north Burma was putting heavy pressure on the Japanese (Map No. 21, page 92). General Stilwell's column had gained 35 miles and was fighting just north of Inkangahtawng, 20 miles from Kamaing. In the Irrawaddy Valley, 45 miles north of Myitkyina, British-led Kachin and Gurkha forces were fighting south toward a large supply base at Nsopzup, having captured the enemy forward base at Sumprabum. To the southeast of Myitkyina, in the Yunnan province of China, Marshal Wei Li-lung was massing Chinese divisions for an offensive in May across the Salween River.

With the enemy's salient in north Burma threatened by attacks from three directions, his communications were imperiled by a blow from the rear. General Wingate's [18] 3 Indian Division had cut the main enemy supply route well south of the Kamaing-Myitkyina battle area. Four of his brigades had been flown into Burma from Manipur; a fifth had made it overland from Ledo to Mohnyin. Operating in 26 columns of 400 men each, the division had set up a block on 16 March at Mawlu, 80 miles south of Myitkyina on the single railroad into north Burma. This left the Japanese with water transport up the Irrawaddy as their principal means of supply.

Taking advantage of these developments, General Stilwell planned to continue his drive down the Mogaung corridor toward Kamaing, with the Chinese 65th Regiment protecting the right flank of the

---

[18] General Wingate was killed in a plane crash on 25 March, and Maj. Gen. W. D. A. Lentaigne became commander of the 3 Indian Division.

Chinese 22d Division as before. For the third time, the 5307th Composite Unit (Provisional) was to take part in a wide flanking move to the east of the main effort. This was to be the most difficult of the Marauders' missions; they were to strike at Myitkyina itself, the chief objective of the campaign. Myitkyina was the principal Japanese base for defense of Burma from the north. Situated 170 air miles southeast of Ledo, it was the northernmost point of a railroad from Rangoon and was also the head of navigation on the Irrawaddy River. It lay in the proposed path of the Ledo Road, some 170 air miles north of the Burma Road junction with the railway at Lashio. The Marauders' surprise thrust deep into enemy-held territory would, if successful, effectually dispose of the principal air base from which Japanese aircraft had menaced American transport planes flying supplies to China. It would also deprive the enemy of an important stronghold, center of·an extensive military framework, and would quickly paralyze all Japanese operations radiating from Myitkyina.

The Force and the Mission

The strike at Myitkyina would test the limits of the Marauders' staying powers. Since 9 February they had marched and fought through 500 miles of exceedingly difficult country. After Nhpum Ga the troops were physically worn out. During most of the 80-day period they had lived on "K" rations. Leeches had caused many so-called "Naga sores," and nearly all of the men had suffered to some extent from dysentery and fevers. However, Myitkyina, where an all-weather airfield would greatly aid in the supply of the troops under General Stilwell's command and hasten the success of his campaign, was worth every effort.

The 5307th Composite Unit (Provisional) had lost about 700 men killed, wounded, or sick. Of this number the 2d Battalion alone had lost about 460, and there were no American replacements in the theater to fill out the Marauder ranks. To provide strength enough for the third mission, General Stilwell decided to reinforce General Merrill with Kachin and Chinese troops, giving his command a total strength of about 7,000 for the Myitkyina operation.

A complete reshuffling of personnel in the 2d Battalion was necessary, for the·casualties which it had sustained, especially at Nhpum

K FORCE MEN *exchange cigarettes for Japanese money.*

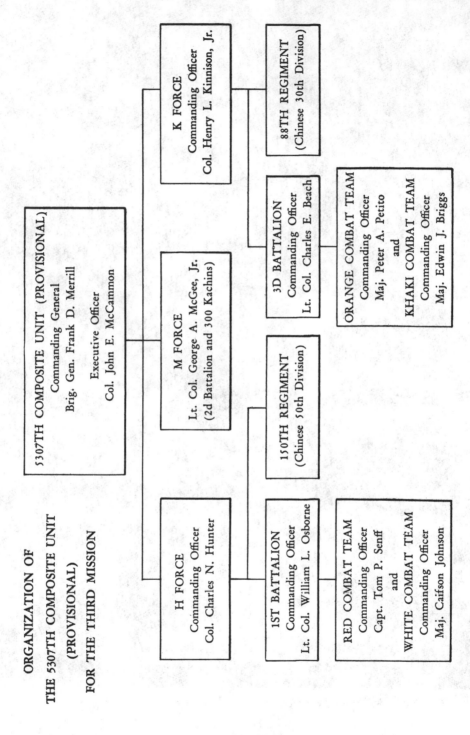

ORGANIZATION OF
THE 5307TH COMPOSITE UNIT
(PROVISIONAL)
FOR THE THIRD MISSION

5307TH COMPOSITE UNIT (PROVISIONAL)
Commanding General
Brig. Gen. Frank D. Merrill
Executive Officer
Col. John E. McCammon

K FORCE
Commanding Officer
Col. Henry L. Kinnison, Jr.

88TH REGIMENT
(Chinese 30th Division)

M FORCE
Lt. Col. George A. McGee, Jr.
(2d Battalion and 300 Kachins)

3D BATTALION
Commanding Officer
Lt. Col. Charles E. Beach

ORANGE COMBAT TEAM
Commanding Officer
Maj. Peter A. Petito
and
KHAKI COMBAT TEAM
Commanding Officer
Maj. Edwin J. Briggs

150TH REGIMENT
(Chinese 50th Division)

H FORCE
Commanding Officer
Col. Charles N. Hunter

1ST BATTALION
Commanding Officer
Lt. Col. William L. Osborne

RED COMBAT TEAM
Commanding Officer
Capt. Tom P. Senff
and
WHITE COMBAT TEAM
Commanding Officer
Maj. Caifson Johnson

Ga, seriously disrupted its combat-team organization. The remaining men, about one-half the original number, were formed into two rifle companies, one heavy weapons company, and a battalion headquarters company, which included an intelligence and reconnaissance platoon, a pioneer and demolition platoon, and a communications platoon. Three hundred Kachin guerrillas were attached to the battalion, and the group, commanded by Colonel McGee, was designated as M Force (Chart, page 96).

The 1st and 3d Battalions retained their original tactical formation of two combat teams each. The 1st Battalion and the Chinese 150th Regiment, 50th Division, combined to form H Force. Colonel Hunter was given command of this force, with Colonel Osborne remaining in charge of the Marauder element. Similarly the 3d Battalion and the Chinese 88th Regiment, 30th Division, became K Force under Col. Henry L. Kinnison, Jr. Colonel Beach continued to be commander of the 3d Battalion. To H Force was assigned a battery of 75-mm pack howitzers of the Chinese 22d Division; to K Force, the battery of the 5307th. General Merrill, recovered for the time being from his illness, returned to headquarters at Naubum. He appointed Col. John E. McCammon as his executive officer.

On 27 April when the three Marauder forces were organized and ready for the third mission, General Stilwell flew in to Naubum to make final arrangements with General Merrill for the operation, with the airfield at Myitkyina as the first objective (Map No. 22, page 98). The same day General Merrill issued orders to the forces for their movement toward Myitkyina. Both H Force and K Force would move northward from Naubum to Taikri, then head east across the main Kumon Range and south to Ritpong. From Ritpong they would continue south through foothills to Seingheing at the edge of the Myitkyina plain.

General Merrill instructed M Force, still operating near Samlugahtawng, to patrol the Senjo Ga—Hkada Ga area and to block any attempted Japanese advance along the Tanai from the south. This would screen the southern flank during the first stage of the advance.

From the Tanai to the Hpungin Valley

On 28 April K Force moved north to Taikri and turned eastward from the Tanai Valley into the mountains (Map No. 22, page 98).

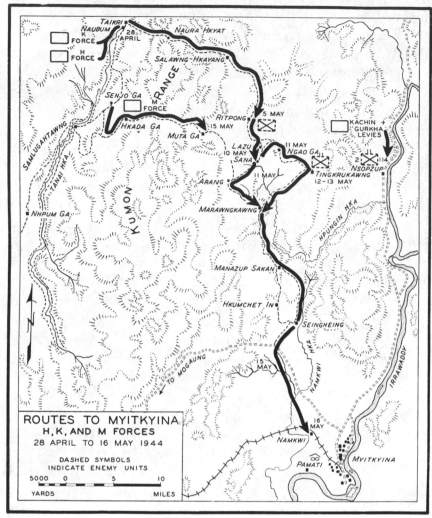

ROUTES TO MYITKYINA
H, K, AND M FORCES
28 APRIL TO 16 MAY 1944

DASHED SYMBOLS
INDICATE ENEMY UNITS

5000 0   5   10
YARDS   MILES

H Force followed 2 days later. About one-fifth of the 65-mile trip
to Myitkyina was over the Kumon Range, rising in this area to over
6,000 feet. The trail across the hills had not been used in 10 years
and was reported to be impassable. Capt. William A. Laffin together
with 2d Lt. Paul A. Dunlap had started off ahead of K Force. With
them went 30 Kachin soldiers and 30 coolies to repair the worst
places on the route.

The monsoon season was commencing. The sky was so cloudy
that air drops became very difficult. Rain fell every day, and the
damp heat was stifling. In some places the trail was so steep that

STARTING ACROSS THE KUMON RANGE, *the Marauders break their climb over the steep trail.*

footholds had to be cut for the pack animals; in others the animals had to be unloaded and their burdens manhandled up precipitous inclines. Occasionally no path of any sort could be found, despite the work of Captain Laffin's advance group. Even the mules slipped on the uncertain footing of the hillsides and plunged to their death in valleys far below. Khaki Combat Team, which was in the lead, lost

MAP NO. 23

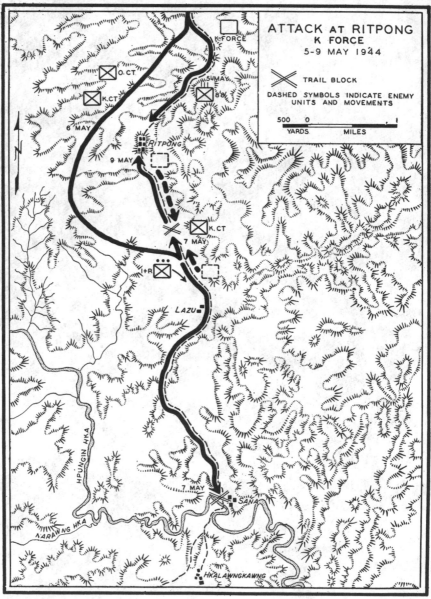

15 of its pack animals and their loads of ammunition and weapons; Orange Combat Team, next in the column, lost 5.

For 5 or 6 days the two forces toiled up and down through the Kumon ridges. Upon reaching Naura Hkyat, they received a report that enemy soldiers were in the vicinity. The I and R Platoon of Khaki Combat Team went forward to block the trails at Salawng-Hkayang. No Japanese were encountered there, but a patrol from the 1st Battalion of the Chinese 88th Regiment, heading southward toward Ritpong, brushed with the enemy on the east flank of the marching column. The Japanese were believed to be holding Ritpong in considerable strength.

Ritpong

On 5 May the leading elements of K Force reached a trail junction just over a mile north of Ritpong (Map No. 23, page 100). Colonel Kinnison decided on an enveloping attack and sent a strong patrol from Khaki Combat Team to prepare an approach to the village from the rear. According to information received, there was a trail which encircled Ritpong to the west and joined another trail south of the village. No such trail was found, so the patrol was forced to start cutting a path through the jungle. The main units of Khaki Combat Team took over the task of chopping trail at daybreak on 6 May, and, after working all day, they emerged on the track south of the village. Orange Combat Team was following close behind. Meanwhile, the Chinese 88th Regiment had unsuccessfully attacked Ritpong from the north.

At 0530 on 7 May, while Orange Combat Team remained at the point where it had bivouacked the previous night, Khaki Combat Team began to close in on Ritpong from the south. At a trail fork only a short distance from the start, a Japanese scout went by without seeing the American advance elements. Khaki Combat Team placed a block at the fork and reconnoitered. A combat patrol, investigating a group of huts within 300 or 400 yards, discovered an enemy outpost engaged in cooking a meal, but the enemy got away as the result of a premature shot. A squad of Japanese coming south from Ritpong was wiped out at the trail block. However, when Khaki Combat Team attempted to push on toward Ritpong it was checked by an enemy machine-gun position that dominated the trail.

Since the Chinese 88th Regiment was making progress north of Ritpong, Colonel Kinnison was content to have the Marauders do no more than block the village from the south. To avoid any surprise attack at the rear of the Marauder teams, he sent an I and R Platoon southward to establish a block at Sana. North of Lazu this platoon ran into a well-protected Japanese supply train which was moving up toward Ritpong. A hot fight ensued. The platoon scattered the Japanese, who fled eastward; they dropped supplies that were later retrieved by K Force.

During the night of 7/8 May, the Japanese tried to break out of Ritpong and twice attacked south against Khaki Combat Team. Coming down the trail, the Japanese made good targets for waiting Marauder machine guns and suffered heavily during both attacks. The enemy used smoke grenades in this effort.

On 8 May the 88th Regiment again attacked the north edge of Ritpong. Orange and Khaki Combat Teams, from their positions south of the town, laid down a barrage of mortar fire to support the drive, but it failed. The following day the village was finally entered. Leaving the Chinese to mop up, the Marauders marched south to Lazu where they established a protective trail block and bivouacked.

Diversion at Tingkrukawng

During the delay at Ritpong, H Force had caught up with K Force, and on 10 May both were at Lazu, about 35 miles northwest of Myitkyina (Map No. 22, page 98). Less than 20 miles to the east, the Japanese in considerable strength were resisting British-led Kachin and Gurkha levies in their drive toward the enemy supply base at Nsopzup. As a result of the engagement at Ritpong, the enemy had learned of the presence of an American unit in the Hpungin Valley, and the Marauders would therefore need to screen their eastern flank. To this end, K Force was to feint toward Nsopzup, occupy the attention of the enemy troops in that vicinity, and thus protect the rear of H Force in its advance for a surprise assault on the Myitkyina air strip.

Early on the morning of 11 May, K Force struck out toward Ngao Ga. The trail ran up and down steep inclines, and the day was the hottest the Marauders had known. Many of the men collapsed from weakness and exhaustion. At 0950 the next day, K Force ran into Japanese, estimated to be a platoon in strength, about 400 yards northwest of the village of Tingkrukawng (Map No. 24, below). Orange Combat Team attacked without delay. As the attack developed, the enemy strength was revealed to be approximately a reinforced battalion, and the Marauders were soon pinned to the ground. Khaki Combat Team, to the rear of Orange Combat Team, supplied mortar support. Orange built up its line, but the going was hard.

A company from the Chinese 88th Regiment was dispatched to cut a trail around to the right, find the Japanese position, and attack the enemy left flank. This attempt failed, for the Chinese ran into heavy opposition and suffered many casualties. Orange Combat Team worked its way to high ground on both sides of the trail. The men found that the Japanese held commanding ground on the opposite side of the village, with dug-in gun positions dominating the approaches.

That night Colonel Kinnison conferred with his commanders. He ordered Khaki Combat Team under Major Briggs to make a circling movement east of the village to hit the enemy from the rear, as Orange

MAP NO. 24

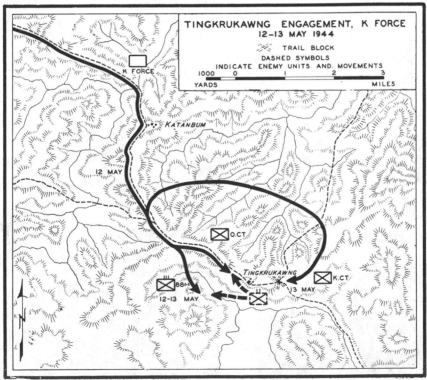

Combat Team pushed straight down the trail. To effect this maneuver, Khaki Combat Team had to cut a trail through the jungle.

At 0615 on 13 May the members of Khaki Combat Team began their task. By noon they had cut their way to a point where precipitous slopes stretched up toward their objective east of the village. The country was so rough that the Marauders could take along neither their animals nor their heavy weapons. With great difficulty the outfit managed to inch its way up the incline. Reaching the crest, the men discovered that the Japanese had constructed a heavy block along the trail. A Japanese patrol from the block tried to work around the

THE MYITKYINA AIR STRIP *was peppered with bomb craters when H Force captured it. (Aerial photograph was taken from 9,300 feet.)*

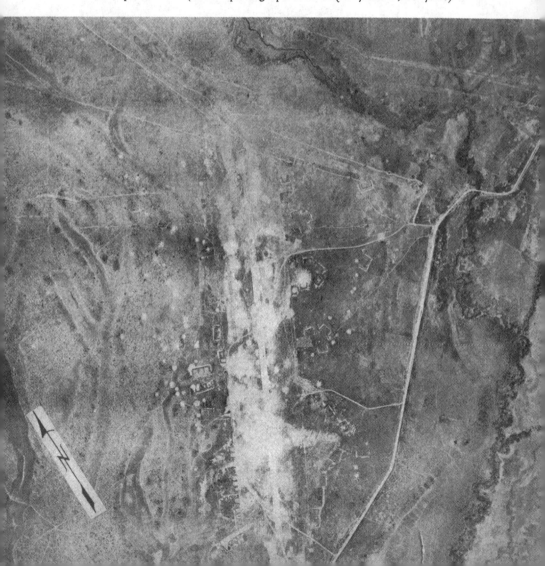

Marauders' right flank and attack their rear, but was checked by two of the combat team's platoons.

Khaki Combat Team was unable to bypass the trail block and get closer to Tingkrukawng. The maneuver yielded one advantage: from a rise in the ground Major Briggs could see Japanese positions in the village and directed Orange Combat Team's mortar fire on them. By 1645 the troops of Khaki Combat Team had used all their ammunition. They had been without food all that day. Since dropping supplies to them was impossible, Colonel Kinnison ordered Major Briggs to withdraw. The evacuation of wounded slowed the withdrawal, which was already made very difficult by darkness.

A Chinese battalion, sent around to the southwest of Tingkrukawng to replace the company which had failed in its attack on the Japanese left flank, achieved no better results. Orange Combat Team's frontal attack was not making any progress.

The Japanese were now receiving reinforcements from the east; furthermore, the operation had provided sufficient diversion to allow H Force to get well under way in its march south. The Marauders had little to gain by continuing the attack, and Colonel Kinnison decided to break off the engagement. He withdrew his troops under the protection of an artillery barrage fired by K Force's guns from Katanbum. Turning southwest on the trail to Marawngkawng, Kinnison's command pushed toward the route already taken by H Force. Marauder casualties in the engagement at Tinkrukawng were 8 killed and 21 wounded. Chinese casualties were heavier.

H Force's Attack on Myitkyina Air Strip

After 11 May, during the time K Force was engaged at Tingkrukawng, H Force was on its way toward Myitkyina (Map No. 22, page 98). From Lazu Colonel Hunter and his men proceeded southward along the trail through Marawngkawng, Manazup Sakan, and Seingheing. After crossing the motor road southwest of Seingheing the force was guided by a Kachin trained by OSS Detachment 101. He led them on a devious course through paddy fields and jungle in order to reach Myitkyina without being seen by either Japanese or natives. At 2030 on 15 May, just as the force reached the upper Namkwi River about 15 miles from the objective, the guide, Nauiyang Nau, was bitten by a poisonous snake. He tried to go on, but within a short time his foot was badly swollen, and he was too sick to move. Without his guidance, the Marauders would have had difficulty finding their way in the dark through the intricate maze of paths. Captain Laffin and Lieutenant Dunlap slashed the spot where the fangs had penetrated Nau's foot and for 2 hours sucked poison from the incision. By 0230 the Kachin was able to mount Colonel Hunter's horse and continue leading until the column reached its destination for the night.

After a brief rest, H Force resumed its march at noon on 16 May and again crossed the Namkwi River, south of the village of Namkwi. So far only two natives had seen the column, and they had been taken along with the force in order to prevent their alerting the enemy. Only 4 miles now from the Myitkyina air strip, Colonel Hunter took more precautions to keep the movement of his force unknown. With the help of the Kachin guerrillas, his men rounded up all the inhabitants of Namkwi, some of whom were known to be of doubtful loyalty, and confined them within H Force's lines until the next morning. The force at this time cut neither the railroad nor the telegraph line, wishing to maintain secrecy about its arrival so close to the airfield.

Colonel Hunter set the time for the attack on the airfield at 1000, 17 May (Map No. 25, page 107). His plan was for the 1st Battalion of the 5307th, under Colonel Osborne, to lead the Chinese 150th Regiment to the southwest end of the field and leave the regiment to attack the strip at that point. Osborne and his men were then to push southwest to the ferry terminal at Pamati. By taking this terminal, the Marauders would control the nearest crossing of the Irrawaddy River. Colonel Hunter's plan for the attack on the air strip was based on the knowledge that because of recent strafing of the field, the Japanese habitually withdrew during daylight to positions in the thick scrub and bamboo clumps at some distance from the strip. In addition, from intelligence brought back by a six-man patrol under Sgt. Clarence E. Branscomb of White Combat Team, Colonel Hunter knew how many Japanese troops and Burmese workmen were about the strip on 16 May.

The attack came off exactly as scheduled. Colonel Osborne left the Chinese 150th Regiment to carry out its part of the mission and, with his Marauders, hastened to Pamati. By 1100 he had taken the village

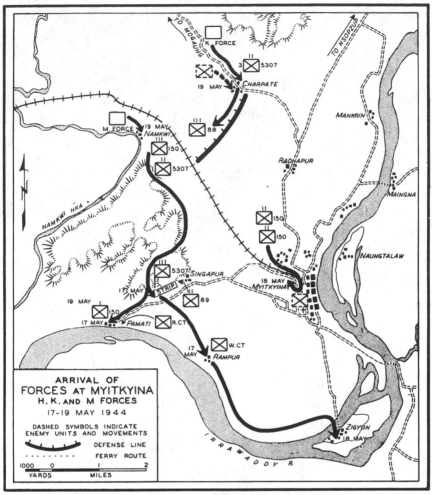

ARRIVAL OF
FORCES AT MYITKYINA
H. K. AND M FORCES
17-19 MAY 1944

DASHED SYMBOLS INDICATE
ENEMY UNITS AND MOVEMENTS

DEFENSE LINE
FERRY ROUTE

1000   0   1   2
YARDS   MILES

and ferry. Red Combat Team was instructed to hold the ferry site, and White Combat Team was sent back to the air strip, where it received orders from Colonel Hunter to seize Zigyun, main ferry point for Myitkyina. At 1700 Osborne and White Combat Team left the air strip and moved southeast to the Irrawaddy River in close proximity to Rampur. There they bivouacked for the night in position to move on Zigyun next morning.

Meanwhile the attack on the airfield by the 150th Regiment had made good progress. The strip was not strongly defended, and the Chinese thrust had come as a complete surprise to the enemy.

Throughout the day sporadic fighting went on in widely separated spots around the airfield, but by noon the field was in Allied hands.

Reinforcements for H Force

When no Japanese reinforcements appeared at the air strip on 17 May, Colonel Hunter concluded that the enemy did not hold Myitkyina in strength. Intelligence reports confirmed his assumption, so he decided to press home the advantage of his surprise assault by attempting to take the city. It was inevitable that the Japanese would soon reinforce their garrison from troops within close reach of the city. The question for Colonel Hunter was whether he or the enemy could build up strength the quicker.

Immediately after capturing the air strip Colonel Hunter radioed General Merrill asking for more troops and supplies. The strip was ready to receive transport planes, which could deliver without loss cargoes 30 percent greater than could be loaded for air drops. Light motor transport and supplies too bulky or too heavy for parachute dropping could now be brought in. The Chinese 89th Regiment, waiting on rear fields, was ordered to leave for Myitkyina, and one battalion arrived by air from Ledo late in the afternoon. Simultaneously Colonel Hunter sent an urgent request to M and K Forces for their assistance. Each force was about a 2 days' trip from Myitkyina. M Force had already moved eastward over the Kumon Range and was at Arang when Colonel McGee received Hunter's call. The force started southward as soon as possible and covered the distance of more than 30 miles by forced marches. K Force had just reached Hkumchet In, about 20 miles north of Myitkyina, when Colonel Hunter's message came over the radio. Colonel Kinnison also ordered his column to continue without delay to assist H Force.

Preliminary Assault on Myitkyina

Immediately on learning of the success at the airfield, General Merrill flew in and established his headquarters (Map No. 25, page 107). His second-in-command, Colonel McCammon, ordered Colonel Hunter to attack the city with the disengaged portion of H Force. One battalion of the Chinese 89th Regiment, which had arrived from Ledo, would defend the air strip while two battalions of the 150th

Regiment attacked Myitkyina. The other battalion of the 150th Regiment would be in reserve at the strip. White Combat Team, near Rampur, would continue toward Zigyun to secure the ferry crossing south of the city. If Red Combat Team held the ferry crossing at Pamati, two of the three approaches to Myitkyina from the south would be under the control of H Force.

Early on the morning of 18 May, White Combat Team troops took possession of Rampur where they found several warehouses filled with clothing and other supplies. Colonel Osborne then moved on to Zigyun. His team occupied the town without any opposition by 1000 and took several Burmese prisoners. Defensive positions were being prepared when Osborne radioed to Colonel Hunter for further instructions. Hunter informed him that a company of Chinese was on the way to relieve White Combat Team, which was to report back to the airfield the moment the Chinese arrived. However, the relief of White Combat Team was considerably delayed as the Chinese unit engaged several groups of Japanese stragglers en route and did not reach Zigyun until 48 hours later. The Chinese dug in nine times in 5 miles.

The two battalions of the Chinese 150th Regiment attacked Myitkyina during the 18th from the north. After taking the railroad station, they became involved in confused fighting and had to retire to a line about 800 yards west of the town. There they dug in.

Meanwhile, K Force was closing in on Myitkyina from the north. About 8 miles from the city the guides leading Kinnison and his men lost their way in the darkness, and K Force bivouacked where they were for the night. Daylight on the 19th disclosed the Myitkyina-Mogaung motor road within 50 yards of their perimeter, and they pushed on along it. When General Merrill learned that K Force was coming in on the road, he radioed Colonel Kinnison to attack and secure Charpate. The village was taken during the morning without appreciable Japanese resistance. The 3d Battalion dug in around the village while the Chinese 88th Regiment moved to the southwest on a line extending roughly from the vicinity of Charpate to the railroad. Kinnison ordered the 3d Battalion to block the Mogaung road and send patrols to block all trails converging on Charpate.

The village stood in the midst of a flat area surrounded by rice paddies. Four or five hundred yards to the northwest the ground rose slightly and was covered with a dense growth of scrub and vines.

In preparing its defensive position, the 3d Battalion overlooked the importance of this high ground. On 19 May the battalion was hit from the northwest by small bands of Japanese who were trying to get into Myitkyina via the Mogaung road. However, none of these engagements was serious.

To the southwest of Charpate, General Merrill was building up a force along the Namkwi River. On 19 May Red Combat Team was relieved at the Pamati ferry by a company of the Chinese 150th Regiment, and the team took up a position on the Namkwi River south of the town. During the evening M Force reached Namkwi. McGee and his men were weak and ill from hunger, for the supplies of food which they had anticipated during the trip south from Arang had not been dropped. After getting food from H Force, McGee's unit was able to outpost Namkwi and patrol to the west and southwest.

General Merrill's forces were now so placed that Japanese reinforcements could reach Myitkyina only from across the Irrawaddy River to the east or along the Myitkyina-Mankrin or Myitkyina-Radhapur roads from the north. The Allied troops were disposed in a semicircle covering all approaches from the northwest, west, southwest, and south. So far, enemy activity was slight in this area. Even at the airfield the continual sniping did not prevent the planes from landing with an ever increasing amount of supplies. If General Merrill retained these positions, he could make a coordinated attack on Myitkyina.

For this purpose he was forming a Myitkyina Task Force, which involved reshuffling of all the units under his command. H and K Forces were dissolved; the Marauder battalions were once more combined under Colonel Hunter; and the Chinese regiments operated as separate units. After this reorganization General Merrill, again ill, had to be evacuated, and Colonel McCammon took over command.

Checkmate

The Myitkyina Task Force was not able to undertake its mission. Instead, a sudden reversal of fortune saw the Allied forces, during the last 10 days of May, thrown back on a defensive struggle to hold the air strip (Map No. 26, page 111). Despite the Marauders' effort to cover main approaches to Myitkyina, the Japanese had been able to reinforce the garrison: an estimated 3,000 to 4,000 enemy had come in from the Nsopzup, Mogaung, and even the Bhamo areas. The

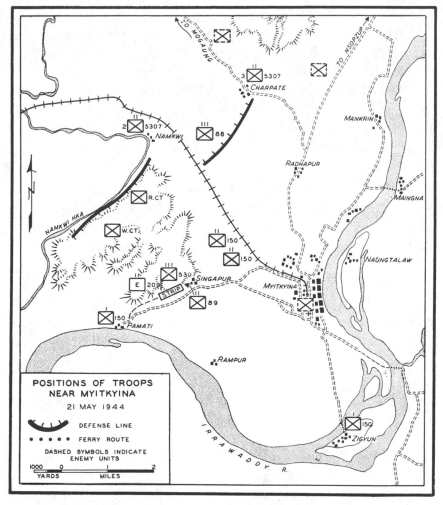

POSITIONS OF TROOPS
NEAR MYITKYINA

21 MAY 1944

⌣ DEFENSE LINE

• • • • FERRY ROUTE

DASHED SYMBOLS INDICATE
ENEMY UNITS

1000   0   1   2
YARDS   MILES

Japanese had built up more strength at Myitkyina than the Allies and by 23 May were passing over to the offensive.

The tired Allied forces seemed pitifully inadequate to deal with a strong enemy counterattack. If the Japanese could recapture the airfield, the American and Chinese troops in the Myitkyina area would be left with no way of escape except the jungle trail over which they had come, and they were in no condition for such an ordeal. The fruits of the brilliant campaign were at stake. The most drastic measures were justifiably taken to collect a force adequate to defend the airfield. Reluctantly the higher command directed that evacuation of sick and exhausted Marauders be held to an absolute minimum.

111

Requests were sent to the camp at Dinjan for Marauders convalescing in hospitals after evacuation from Burma as casualties. Some 200 convalescents were rushed to Myitkyina, but about 50 of these men were judged unfit for combat by the doctors at the airfield and were immediately sent back. A group of replacements who had just arrived in India and were at Ramgarh for training were also rushed in by air. These desperate expedients warded off the immediate peril; then Marauder reinforcements, with the 209th Engineer Combat Battalion, strengthened the Allied forces at Myitkyina and kept the Japanese from attacking the airfield.

The enemy concentrated his attacks north of the field, where the first evidence of difficulty showed on 21 May. The 3d Battalion of the 5307th had left Charpate at 1000 to reach the road junction north of Radhapur. Just short of the junction, Beach encountered a prepared enemy position. Tight bands of automatic fire directed over level terrain pinned his force to the ground. The battalion dug in. During the night the Japanese came down the Mogaung road through Charpate to attack the 3d Battalion's rear, but our artillery fire drove them off. In the morning Beach withdrew his battalion to the original position at Charpate and resumed his patrolling.

At 2200 on the night of 23 May a battalion of Japanese launched an attack on Charpate from the rise northeast of the town. Beach's force had been depleted by sickness, and some of his men were out on patrol. The Japanese attack penetrated the 3d Battalion's position early in the action. From the south 75-mm artillery supported the battalion's defense. The Marauders, fighting stubbornly, repelled the attack, but they suffered severe casualties. On the morning of 24 May at 0935, the 3d Battalion had to face still another attack. The fight was going badly when Hunter ordered Beach to break contact with the enemy and move to the railroad, 2½ miles to the south. The Japanese occupied Charpate and held it in force as soon as the 3d Battalion withdrew.

Two days later the Japanese, supported by mortar fire, attacked Namkwi heavily, and the 2d Battalion pulled back to a ridge about halfway to Myitkyina. The Japanese then occupied Namkwi and fortified it strongly. They had now taken over two of the towns on the main approaches to Myitkyina.

On 27 May Company C of the 209th Engineer Combat Battalion

was attached to the 2d Battalion. McGee was ordered to reconnoiter the Charpate area and to attempt reaching Radhapur once again. Just south of Charpate, McGee's forces were attacked. The Japanese were not present in great strength, but the 2d Battalion was so wasted by fatigue, dysentery, malaria, and malnutrition that the unit was not effective for combat. During the engagement several men went to sleep from exhaustion. Colonel McGee himself lost consciousness three times and between relapses directed the battalion from an aid station. Although the attack was beaten off, McGee became convinced that his troops were unfit for further employment and asked to have them relieved as soon as possible.

* * *

For most of the Marauders, this was the last action at Myitkyina. Both the 1st and the 3d Battalions were back near the air strip, and neither one had enough men fit for combat to be a fighting force.

When Myitkyina itself did not fall on 18 May, it was apparent that a larger force was required to besiege the city, a task for which the Marauder unit had not been trained and which it was not strong enough to accomplish. By June the unit was expended. Only 1,310 men had reached Myitkyina, and of this number 679 were evacuated to rear hospitals between 17 May and 1 June. Allied reinforcements arrived to carry on the fight, and about 200 men of the 1st Battalion remained in the area until the fall of Myitkyina on 3 August. The remnants of this force took part in the final attack on the town.

The Distinguished Unit Citation awarded to the unit summarized its campaign:

"After a series of successful engagements in the Hukawng and Mogaung Valleys of North Burma, in March and April 1944, the unit was called on to lead a march over jungle trails through extremely difficult mountain terrain against stubborn resistance in a surprise attack on Myitkyina. The unit proved equal to its task and after a brilliant operation on 17 May 1944 seized the airfield at Myitkyina, an objective of great tactical importance in the campaign, and assisted in the capture of the town of Myitkyina on 3 August 1944."

Annex No. 1: Casualties

CASUALTIES FOR THE 5307TH COMPOSITE UNIT (PROVISIONAL)
February to June, 1944

	Casualties	Percent of casualties	
		Actual	Estimated before operation
BATTLE CASUALTIES:			
Battle deaths	93		
Nonbattle deaths	30		
Wounded in action	[19]293		
Missing in action	8		
SUBTOTAL	424	14	35
DISEASE CASUALTIES:			
Amoebic dysentery	503		
Typhus fever	149		
Malaria	[20]296		
Psychoneurosis	72		
Miscellaneous fevers (approx.)	950		
SUBTOTAL	1970	66	50
TOTAL	2394	80	85

[19] These are the official figures of The Adjutant General's battle casualty roster for hospitalized wounded. Many cases of light battle casualties were not evacuated but treated by unit surgeons and consequently not reported in hospital returns. Therefore, complete statistics are not obtainable. The actual number of wounded at Nhpum Ga alone exceed the official total for the entire campaign.

[20] 296 is the number of malaria cases evacuated. Nearly every member of the force had it in more or less severe form.

114

Annex No. 2: Decorations

THE FOLLOWING LIST of decorations is based on the best records available to date but is not necessarily complete. It does not include the Purple Heart. Posthumous awards are indicated by an asterisk (*).

DISTINGUISHED SERVICE CROSS

1st Lt. Melvin R. Blair
Pfc. Marvin H. Dean
Pfc. Willard J. D. Lilly

Pfc. Herman Manuel
Pvt. Howard T. Smith
Tec. 5 Russell G. Wellman

LEGION OF MERIT

S/Sgt. John A. Acker
Capt. Charles E. Darlington
  (British Army)

S/Sgt. Roy H. Matsumoto
Maj. Melvin A. Schudmak
T/Sgt. Francis Wonsowicz

SILVER STAR

T/Sgt. Edward C. Ammon
Pfc. Marvin H. Anderson
1st Lt. Paul E. Armstrong
M/Sgt. James C. Ballard
Pfc. Earnest C. Banks
Lt. Col. Charles E. Beach
Pfc. Paul R. Bicknell

1st Lt. William Lepore
S/Sgt. Earl Little
S/Sgt. James L. Marsh
Lt. Col. George A. McGee, Jr.
Pvt. Paul V. Michael
*Tec. 4 William H. Miles
1st Lt. Robert C. Newman

Capt. George G. Bonnyman
1st Sgt. Clarence E. Branscomb
Maj. Edwin J. Briggs
*Pfc. Daniel V. Carrigan
S/Sgt. Ellsworth Dalmus
Tec. 4 Lewis Day, Jr.
Pfc. Harold E. Dibble
M/Sgt. Ralph E. Duston
Capt. John R. Fair
Tec. 5 Joseph N. Gomez
Pfc. Everett E. Hudson
Col. Charles N. Hunter
Tec. 5 Emory Jones
Col. Henry L. Kinnison, Jr.

*Pfc. Lambert L. Olson
Pfc. Leonard G. Porath
S/Sgt. Salvadore F. Rapisarda
1st Sgt. Worth E. Rector
S/Sgt. Ernest W. Reid
Sgt. Harold Shoemaker
2d Lt. Winslow B. Stevens
*Tec. 5 Luther E. Sutterfield
2d Lt. John W. Travis
Pvt. Clayton A. Vantol
1st Lt. Victor J. Weingartner
2d Lt. Philip S. Weld
1st Lt. Samuel V. Wilson

SOLDIER'S MEDAL

Capt. John M. Jones, III

BRONZE STAR MEDAL

Capt. John H. Ahrens
Sgt. Clifford Allen
Tec. 5 George J. Anderson
Tec. 5 Eugene F. Arnold
Tec. 5 Louis F. Barberi
Capt. Thomas E. Bogardus
Capt. George G. Bonnyman
S/Sgt. Charles H. Branton
Maj. Edwin J. Briggs
Tec. 4 Robert L. Carr
1st Sgt. Linwood C. Clements
CWO Thomas J. Dalton
Pfc. Claude L. Davis
Maj. Raymond L. Derraux
S/Sgt. John F. Doran
T/Sgt. Woodrow H. Gelander
1st Lt. William C. Grissom
Tec. 5 Koore Hanson

1st Lt. Lawrence V. Lindgren
S/Sgt. Francis K. Luke
S/Sgt. Roy H. Matsumoto
Sgt. Jack V. Mayer
1st Lt. Maurice Metcalf
1st Lt. Edward A. McLogan
Lt. Col. William L. Osborne
S/Sgt. Allen H. Overby
Pfc. Wayne M. Price
Pvt. Paul L. Rogers
Maj. Bernard Rogoff
T/Sgt. Frank Russell
2d Lt. Warren R. Smith
S/Sgt. Charles R. Stewart
Pfc. Milton Susnjer
Pfc. Joseph F. Sweeney
Sgt. Perlee W. Tintary
Pfc. Darrel M. Tomlinson

Maj. Richard W. Healy
2d Lt. George S. Hearn
Maj. George H. Hestad
Capt. James E. T. Hopkins
1st Lt. Theodore Hughes, Jr.
Maj. Caifson Johnson
Sgt. Edward C. Kohler
S/Sgt. Robert B. Kroy
Capt. Kenneth S. Laney
Pfc. Adam J. Lang

Tec. 5 Harland Vadnais
Sgt. Arthur A. Werner, Jr.
1st Lt. Logan E. Weston
1st Lt. Samuel V. Wilson
2d Lt. William E. Woomer
Pfc. Leonard S. Wray
Pfc. Willard F. Yardley
Sgt. Osiride O. Zanardelli
S/Sgt. Jack E. Zosel

OAK LEAF CLUSTER TO SILVER STAR

Lt. Col. Charles E. Beach
S/Sgt. Ellsworth Dalmus

1st Lt. Samuel V. Wilson

INSIGNIA *of the 5307th Composite Unit (Provisional).*

☆ U.S. GOVERNMENT PRINTING OFFICE: 1990 250–874